THE MIRAGE OF TOLERANCE: A

REEVALUATION OF TOLERANCE IN

MEDIEVAL SPAIN, 711-1492

By Adam Manuel

The author hereby grants the American Public University System the right to display these contents for education purposes.

The author assumes total responsibility for meeting the requirements set by United States copyright law for the inclusion of any materials that are not the author's creation or in the public domain.

DEDICATION AND ACKNOWLEDGMENTS

I dedicate this thesis to my father, Eddie Manuel. He has taught me to always follow my dreams and never give up. I would also like to dedicate this to my mother, Shirley Manuel, who is always there to remind me to do my best. Most of all, I would like to dedicate this to God because through him all things are possible.

I wish to thank the members of my committee for their support, patience, and good humor. It was Dr. Mark Bowles with his ever present words of encouragement and guidance that helped me keep up the momentum to finish my thesis. Also, I would like to thank Dr. Heather Thornton for her words of advice and motivation that helped me to keep going further despite the long days of writing and reading required to finish my thesis. I would also like to thank my fellow classmates for their tough, but often useful, advice during the whole writing process.

I have found my coursework throughout the ancient and classical history program to be stimulating and thoughtful, providing me with the tools with which to explore both past and present ideas and issues.

Table of Contents

Table of Figures

CHAPTER I: INTRODUCTION

History only holds true weight in the eyes and souls of those who lived it. For
historians, trying to grasp that same feeling is close to impossible the older the history
becomes. For example, history books describe in a simple sentence that on March 31,
1492, Christian Spain formally issued a decree telling all Jews living in the kingdom that
they must convert to Christianity or leave and never come back. Unfortunately, a simple
sentence does not truly do service to the breadth of what Christian Spain was stating with
this decree. The Jews of Spain were instructed to pack up the necessities of life and
never return. Imagine the fear, sadness, and hatred that they would feel as they heard the
following lines read from a town crier, "Therefore, we, with the counsel and advice of
prelates, great noblemen of our kingdoms, and other persons of learning and wisdom of
our council, having taken deliberations about this matter, resolve to order the said Jews
and Jewesses of our kingdoms to depart and never to return or come back to them or to
any of them."[1] It is mere presumption to assume that these men and women must have
felt absolutely shocked and stunned. To complicate this matter, many generations of
families had lived under the Muslim emirs and Christian kings of Spain with some slight
degree of tolerance.[2] It is overly optimistic to jump to the conclusion that Christians,
Muslims, and Jews lived next to each other, sharing culture and beliefs and having

---

[1] Luis Suárez-Fernádez, ed., Translated by Edward Peters, "Documentos acerca de la expulsion de
los judios," in *Medieval Iberia: Readings from Christian, Muslim, and Jewish Sources,* edited by Olivia
Remie Constable, Second Edition, (Philadelphia, PA: University of Pennsylvania Press, 2012), 511.

rational and unprejudiced discussions on the differences between each other. While it is true that certain aspects of the three religious faiths saw a mixing, adoption, and acceptance of various aspects of each other's cultures, languages, and the very identities of those involved in this situation, it is not enough to boldly claim that complete tolerance existed between the religions. If there was a tolerance to this degree, there would be no record of wars, in-fighting, intrigues, execution, and persecutions between the Christians, Muslims, and Jews that lived in Spain from the years 711 up to the dawn of the Early Modern era in 1492. If tolerance truly existed, Christian Spain would not have expelled the Jews living in Spain in the year 1492. Another sign of this overall intolerance is the fact that ten years later in 1502, Spain formally decreed that all Muslims living in the kingdom of Spain were to "…not dare to arrive or return or be in these our realms or in any part of them, by residence or passing through or any other manner, forever and ever, with the penalty that, if they were to do so and were found to be in our realms and domains or to enter them in any manner, they will incur by this deed, with no other legal trial or sentence or declaration, said penalty of death and confiscation of all their goods for our Chamber of Finance."[3] These two events should create various questions to those studying the period. The idea of one's material possessions, feelings, and desires meaning nothing is hard to fathom. Why have historians for the past century viewed this

---

[3] F. Fernández y González, translated by Dayle Seidenspinner-Nuñez, "Estado social y político de los mudejares de Castilla," in *Medieval Iberia: Readings from Christian, Muslim, and Jewish Sources,* edited by Olivia Remie Constable, (Philadelphia, PA: University of Pennsylvania Press, 2012), 538-539.

era as tolerant? One possible solution would be that much of Europe and the rest of the

western world have a pre-disposition to democracy. Sandra Marquart-Pyatt and Pamela

Paxton state in their article "In Principle and in Practice: Learning Political Tolerance in

Eastern and Western Europe" that a majority of democratic states "require citizens to

tolerate the views and political participation of others...."[4] This would explain why

many historians describe the situation in Medieval Spain as tolerant because they are

seeing it with a Western perspective. As stated previously, it is hard to truly ascertain

what actually happened the older the historical records became. Therefore, to claim that

Christians, Muslims, and Jews lived together in peaceful coexistence because the sources

display it this way is, unfortunately, naïve. Tolerance existed not out of happy

coincidence, but out of the result of careful manipulation of a system that worked

together to create the illusion, or mirage, to not only the people of the time, but most

importantly to historians studying the period of tolerance.

Background and Need

> Of all the lands from the west to the Indies, you, Spain, O sacred and always fortunate
> mother of princes and peoples, are the most beautiful. Rightly are you now the queen of
> all provinces, from which not only the west but also the east borrows its shining light.
> You are the pride and the ornament of the world, the more illustrious part of the earth....[5]

Sandra Marquart-Pyatt and Pamela Paxton, "In Principle and in Practice: Learning Political Tolerance in Eastern and Western Europe," *Political Behavior* 29, no. 1 (March 2007): 90.

[5] Isidore of Seville, translated by Kenneth B. Wolf, "History of the Goths, Vandals, and Suevi," in *Medieval Iberia: Readings from Christian, Muslim, and Jewish Sources*, edited by Olivia Remie Constable, (Philadelphia, PA: University of Pennsylvania Press, 2012), 3.

Isidore of Seville wrote these words in 624 A. D. in his *History of the Goths, Vandals, and Suevi.* In this excerpt, Isidore is describing the amazing beauty and power of the Spanish peninsula. Furthermore, he is discussing the power and importance that Spain has had throughout Spain's long history. These words were written during the reign of the Visigoth leaders of Spain. However, the Visigothic kings were the leaders of just one of the three empires to have possession of Spain before the Spanish finally were able to begin ruling themselves after the conquering of Granada in 1492. Before the Visigoths, the Roman Empire was involved in various aspects of the life of the Iberian Peninsula then known as *Hispania.*[6] In fact two emperors of the Roman Empire came from the areas of Spain, Trajan and Hadrian.[7] Then, after the fall of the Roman Empire to barbarian raiders, the Visigoths eventually took over. They had a short period of rule. In 711 A. D. Spain was conquered by Muslim raiders and began the 782-year period known as Muslim Spain. This, however, is a short exploration of the history of Spain. Before a thorough study of the role of tolerance in Medieval Spain can begin, one must have an adequate grasp of the history of Spain. Without a basic knowledge of the history of Spain, it would be difficult for one to understand the very intricate and sometimes complex culture of the Spanish people. To further give credibility to the arguments in the

---

[6] Raymond Carr, *Spain: A History*, (New York: Oxford University Press, 2000), 25.

[7] Ibid., 34.

research, an explanation of the various aspects of tolerance that existed in Spain from the years 711-1492 follows.

Roman Spain

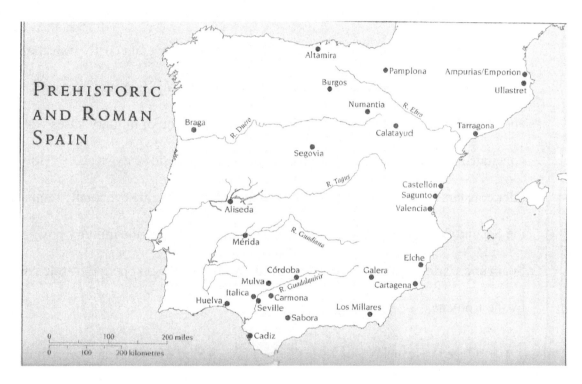

Figure 1: Map of Prehistoric and Roman Spain[8]

Unfortunately, much of the history of prehistoric Spain is highly speculative; therefore, for the purposes of this project much of the history of prehistoric Spain will be overlooked. However, it was with the Roman Republic and Empire that the Iberian Peninsula (Spain) started to be recognized in the texts of the time. One of the first major events that Spain played in the history of the world was the actions involving the Punic

---

[8] Ibid., 22.

Wars. Geographically, southern Spain had a close proximity to the city of Carthage, an important player in the Punic Wars. During the third century B. C., Carthaginians were making their way into the southern borders of Spain and were beginning to establish colonies. This made the Romans jealous.[9] This jealousy eventually resulted in what is known as the First Punic War (264-242 B.C.).[10] In this long and costly war, the Carthaginians were defeated. However, the major generals Hamilcar Barca, Hamsdrubal, and Hannibal worked together to create Spain as a location of military bases which concluded any independence that Spain had in their prehistoric existence.[11] However, after constant antagonism from Hamilcar and his family, Rome eventually retaliated in the Second Punic War (218-201 B.C.).[12] However, this time, the military positions in Spain and Carthage were entirely destroyed. This began a long period of rule and control by the Romans.

Once the Romans took over Spain, a long period of change and growth was seen in the area. Due to Romanization, the people of Spain became more civilized and the inclusion of the Spaniards in Roman life "brought the Hispanic peoples into the mainstream of European civilization, and for the first time, the peninsula was unified

[9] Joseph F. O'Callaghan, *A History of Medieval Spain,* (New York: Cornell University Press, 1975), 27.

[10] Ibid.

[11] Carr, 18; O'Callaghan 27.

[12] O'Callaghan, 27.

under one government."[13] Over the years, Romans utilized consuls and governors to help create political stability in Spain. One of these pivotal and important people behind this stability was Tiberius Gracchus. Historian Raymond Carr describes this era perfectly when he states "Gracchus' work marks a shift from the Spanish provinces being seen merely as theatres of operation towards them being conceived as territorial units."[14] Other than government, the Spaniards learned and adapted their primitive languages into their own version of Latin. Also religions and ideas were adopted from the Romans, and it would eventually contribute to the overall Spanish identity. Unfortunately, as years went by, Spain went in and out of possession by the Roman Empire. Spain became a territory that was fought over because of its important goods and services, and many people saw it as an important source of personal territorial gain. Even more complicating, Spain saw many different incarnations of the organization of Spain. For example, after the Second Punic War, Spain was broken into two pieces, *Hispania Citeror* and *Hispania Ulterior*.[15] However, in approximately 27 B.C., Emperor Augustus broke the peninsula into three parts: Baetica, Lusitania, and Hispania Citerior. This was further complicated in 284 A.D. when Emperor Diocletian broke Spain down into five pieces: Gallaetia, Lusitania, Baetica, Tarraconensis, and Cartaginensis. One can see the

---

[13] Ibid., 28.

[14] Carr, 25.

[15] Ibid., 23.

breakdown of Spain in Figure 2. Medieval Spain, like Roman Spain, was constantly experiencing the change in the borders, laws, and the very identity of its people. As the Reconquista successfully added lands back to Christian Spain, land boundaries were constantly being updated from previous sizes. It was during the rule of the Romans that Christianity was eventually introduced into Spain. Jews had lived in Spain for centuries along with Roman pagans, but the establishment of Spain as a Christian entity was the beginning of the attempt for the many religions to attempt to live together.

Figure 2: Map of Late Roman Spain[16]

---

[16] O'Callaghan, 29.

Eventually in 409 A. D., Spain was invaded by the Alans, Sueves, and the Vandals from the north and slowly fell to their rule.[17] This was the end of the period known as Roman Spain and the beginning of the period commonly referred to as Visigothic Spain.

Visigothic Spain

Figure 3: Visigothic Spain[18]

---

[17] Carr, 288.

[18] O'Callaghan, 45.

Visigothic Spain started and ended the same way, with invasion. Visigothic Spain lasted from the early fifth century until Spain was invaded by Muslim raiders in 711. One can see from Figure 3 that Visigoth Spain was constantly being pressured and invaded from all directions. This created great instability in Spain. One can also see in Figure 3 that Spain was still separated into the same five pieces that it was separated into in Roman Spain. The history of Visigoth Spain is extremely compartmentalized. Nearly the entire first century of Visigothic rule (409-484 A.D.) was comprised of the various northern peoples fighting over control and superiority.[19] However, finally in the years of 466-484 A. D., King Euric completed the conquest of Spain, and once again Spain was controlled by an entity other than itself.[20] Life in Spain can be simply summarized into three categories: religious disputes, persecution, and war. Other than war among themselves, the later Visigoths were at constant war with a newly emerged sect of peoples, the Muslims.

Religiously, Visigothic kings were highly prejudiced in their view of the superiority of the Christian belief over all other beliefs. However, early in Visigothic Spain, the Visigoths prescribed to a controversial brand of Christianity, and it caused many problems with many of the other branches of Christianity in Europe and abroad. This unique version of Christianity was Arian Christianity, and they were supporters of

---

[19] Ibid.

[20] Ibid.

this belief for several centuries. However, in the late sixth century, the Visigoths began

to convert to Catholicism.[21] One of the main reasons for this change was that, in the

Council of Nicaea in 325and at the Third Council of Toledo of 589, Arian Christianity

was condemned as heretical and as a way of bringing unification to the people of

Visigothic Spain.[22] Other than internal disputes over Christianity, the Visigoths were

constantly competing with the Jews who lived in Spain alongside the Christians. It was

during this time that the Jews saw persecution and strict regulations on their lives unseen

until well into the modern-era. In many ways, the Visigothic era was the beginning of the

question of tolerance in Spain. Since the Visigothic Christians were highly prejudiced

against Jews, this period saw a great deal of intolerance toward the Jews. Historian of

Jewish History, Jane S. Gerber describes this period as "…the Visigothic era was a time

of mounting anti-Jewish legislation."[23] The legislation that Gerber is talking about is a

series of strict law codes established by the Visigoths called *Lex Visigothorum*, and it was

a set of laws that the Visigoths felt would adequately control all realms of Spain. These

laws greatly hindered the livelihood of all Jews in Spain and essentially delegated them to

the position of sub-human.[24] For example, one law from the *Lex Visigothorum* states,

---

[21] Olivia Remie Constable, ed., *Modern Iberia: Readings from Christian, Muslim, and Jewish Sources,* Second Edition, (Philadelphia, PA: University of Pennsylvania Press, 2012), 12.

[22] Ibid.

[23] Janes S. Gerber, *The Jews of Spain: A History of the Sephardic Experience,* (NY: The Free Press, 1994), 11.

[24] Constable, 12-26.

"…[d]eservedly therefore Jews, whether baptized or not baptized, are forbidden to give testimony in court."[25] The law then states that any Jew that behaves in a proper manner fitting the standards of the Christian elite, they could give testimony in court with supervision by a Christian lawyer.[26] This would definitely be demeaning and would have greatly affected the lives of the Jews of Visigothic Spain. The only time that they could testify in court was when they "behaved themselves".

Visigothic rule was never entirely stable or secure. Therefore, it is not outside of the realm of possibility to believe that the majority of the years of Visigoth rule was comprised of war and in-fighting. After 484 when Euric established complete control over Spain, up to the conquest of Spain by the Muslims, Spain was constantly fighting within or without. For example, the years 507-583 were nearly eight decades of great hostility and fragility. The year 507 saw the Battle of Vouille, where the Franks successfully rest Gaul from Spain.[27] The years 551-583 saw several revolts from smaller kingdoms within Visigoth Spain which created great hostility and violence in the realm. Other than fighting among themselves, Spain started to fight and skirmish with a people of a new religion. In 622, Muhammad and his followers set up the first *umma* in Medina.[28]

---

[25] Karl Zeumer, ed., "Monumenta Germaniae Historica: legume section I, Leges Visigothorum," In *Medieval Iberia: Readings from Christian, Muslim, and Jewish Sources,* edited by Olivia Remie Constable, second edition, (Philadelphia, PA: University of Pennsylvania Press, 2012), 24.

[26] Ibid.

[27] Carr, 288.

[28] An *umma* is a term meaning a Muslim community; Arthur Goldschmidt, Jr. and Lawrence

From that location, the religion of the Muslims started to spread throughout the Middle East and parts of Africa. From the years 622 to 710, the Muslims spread their religion throughout the Middle East and early Africa, and it was the Berbers of North Africa who eventually conquered Visigoth Spain, essentially by accident.[29] According to the statistics given by historian Joseph F. O'Callaghan, a small force of 400 men sent purely for reconnaissance, ended up conquering southern portions of Spain with little to no resistance.[30] On April 711, Tariq ibn Ziyad and a larger force of approximately 7,000 landed in southern Spain and fought their way toward the Guadelete River where a total combined Muslim force of 12,000 faced off against the Visigoth army on July 19, 711.[31] From this point until the Fall of Granada in 1492, there was some degree of Muslim rule in Spain. The events of Visigoth Spain perfectly tie into the argument proposed in the thesis. It was during the period of Visigoth rule that Spain started experimenting with using laws and warfare to control the people of Spain. Laws that may appear to be out of tolerance and acceptance of the people's beliefs were actually mere mechanisms of the government to control the people.

Davidson, *A Concise History of the Middle East*, tenth edition, (Philadelphia, PA: Westview Press, 2013), 437.

[29] O'Callaghan, 52.

[30] Ibid.

[31] Ibid., 53.

Muslim Spain

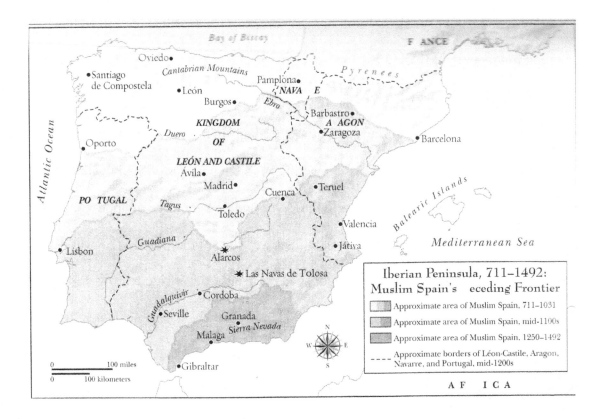

Figure 4: Muslim Spain 711-1492[32]

After the dust settled from the conquest of Spain in 711 by the Muslims, Spain

was once again reorganized. According to Figure 4, one can see that Christian states

were sequestered in northern Spain, and the Muslims possessed all lands below the Duero

River. However, even the history of Muslim Spain is complex and is often made up of

several parts. In the years 711-756 Muslim rulers were in the process of conquering

portions of Spain and systematically adding more land to the vast empire they had built.

[32] Chris Lowney, *A Vanished World: Muslims, Christians, and Jews in Medieval Spain*, (New York: Oxford University Press, 2005), ii.

While the conquest of Spain was in action, there was a violence in the Middle East that

would have a great importance to the history of Spain. That violence was a great

insurrection in which the Umayyads of Damascus were being systematically killed by the

Abbasids. [33] However, luckily one member of the Umayyad family Abd al-Rahman fled

the political persecution of his homeland and escaped to the refuge of Muslim Spain.[34] It

was then after a few minor military endeavors, Abd al-Rahman solidified himself as the

leader of a new capital of Cordoba. O'Callaghan states, "Abd al-Rahman made a

triumphal entry into Cordoba where he was proclaimed emir, transforming Al-Andalus

into an independent kingdom and the new home of the exiled Umayyad dynasty."[35] Then

for nearly two centuries, other than the occasional skirmish with weak Christian kings, or

opposing Muslim rebels, Spain was relatively quiet of major events. However, in 929,

Abd al-Rahman III changed the role of Muslim Spain when he proclaimed himself caliph

instead of emir, which was customary of all of his predecessors.[36] This was a pivotal

move, because religiously, it establishes Abd al-Rahman as a successor in authority of all

Muslims, by Muhammad's instruction. However, this also made the relations between

Christian, Muslim, and Jew tense, as well as with other Muslim groups. From this point

on, there was a rise in more violence and actions of prejudice and hatred toward people of

---

[33] O'Callaghan, 100.

[34] Ibid.

[35] Al-Andalus was the Muslim term for Spain; O'Callaghan, 100-101.

[36] Carr, 289.

other religious beliefs. These feelings were fueled by feelings within and without Spain.

The eleventh century saw the beginning of the Crusades and their various attempts to

solidify Christianity and destroy anything that resembled Islam. In 1086, Muslim Spain

saw the invasion of the Almoravids and their establishment of rule of Muslim Spain.[37]

This was followed in 1148 by the invasion of the Almohads into Muslim Spain, and their

taking control of Muslim Spain from the Almoravids.[38] This also fueled the Christian

north as they started a period of *Reconquista* to take back Spain from Muslims. Then as

the years went by, Christian Spain grew in size as the strength of the Muslim emirs

weakened, and the Christian kings grew in strength. The year 1469 saw the marriage of

King Ferdinand to Isabella, and essentially solidified the actions of the future.[39] Near the

end of the fifteenth century Spain was Christian, except Granada, which stubbornly

retained strength as a Muslim position. Also, in 1478 the Inquisition was established,

according to most historians as a way of ridding Spain of heresies such as Judaism, Islam,

and other forms of blasphemy in the eyes of Spanish society. Finally, in 1492, the

Conquest of Granada was completed, and Spain became a completely Christian kingdom.[40]

This was followed nearly immediately by the expulsion of the Jews from Spain and ten

years later by the expulsion of the Muslims.

---

[37] Ibid., 290.

[38] Ibid.

[39] Ibid., 291.

[40] Ibid.

True Tolerance

One of the main focuses of this project is to understand the role of tolerance in Medieval Spain. Most historians such as María Rosa Menocal, Chris Lowney, Joseph F. O'Callaghan, and Raymond Carr believe that there was some form of tolerance, but they all disagree as to what degree. Therefore, it is vital to clarify what the researcher is referring to when genuine tolerance is discussed in comparison to what other historians have termed tolerance. The researcher proposes that the closest that Spain came to genuine shades of tolerance can be found in situations when religion was actually minimal to non-existent and the people were focused on themselves. One of the first major areas of actual tolerance can be found in business and commerce. There are numerous sources that clearly show citizens of different religious backgrounds being tolerant of each other. However, they were not being tolerant because they cared about the other's religion or appreciated the religion. Instead these people were solely interested in furthering the strength of their business and making as much money as possible. This scenario related to all religions, but the Jews were most successful when it came to this form of tolerance. It was this form of tolerance that allowed Jews at certain points in Medieval Spain to rise to become financially wealthy, and even to lead in government situations. Another way in which tolerance existed can be found in the actions of intellectual exchange. Muslim Spain saw a large interest in the ancient texts, and during this time many of the old Roman and Greek sources were saved from becoming forgotten to time by huge endeavors by Muslim, Christian, and Jewish historians. The caliphs of Spain were huge supporters of education, and it is proven by the astronomical number of libraries that existed in Muslim Spain. One sign of tolerance in this aspect is the idea of translation. The Muslims would find an old Latin work, and then with Muslims and Jews would go about translating them into the respective languages of the people of Spain. There was also a tolerance that did exist in Muslim Spain that was not visible at the time, but upon retrospect it is obvious that there were certain aspects of each culture that blended to form modern Spanish identity. One of the largest signs is the Spanish language. Spanish, a Romance language, was molded by its close proximity with Arabic and Jewish vocabulary, and inevitably certain words were adopted into the vernacular. Similar forms of adoption can also be seen in the architecture of the time period. Muslims would design Christian churches in Spain and Byzantine Christians designed mosques in Syria, not because they loved each other, but because they were being paid to do so. Artistically, Muslim Spain saw a huge flowering of poetry and literature, and it was during this time that Spaniards started to imitate the styles of each other, and before long, there was a cornucopia of different styles that all had a Muslim aspect. Therefore, there are certain aspects of tolerance that did exist in Medieval Spain. However, where historians are in error in their discussion of these topics is the idea of why. Muslims and Christians were not translating texts because they truly valued the information entirely, but because they were profiting from it. This translation allowed them to live a normal life in the time. Also, due to the regulations that required Christians, Muslims, and Jews to live in such close proximity, it was inevitable for the languages, culture, arts, and architecture of those living together to start to resemble each other. It was the natural process of the people living in such close proximity to each other.

This has been a short and abbreviated look at the history of Spain, as well as a look at what true tolerance existed in Spain. It shows that Spain has had a long and complex history from the period of pre-history to the expulsion of the Jews in 1492. Before Spain was finally able to start ruling themselves in the late fifteenth and early sixteenth century, Spain had been in some form a subject to the Romans, the Visigoths, and finally the Muslim emirs and caliphs. From the Romans the Spaniards went from being a territory of simple farmers to people of learning and importance. From the Romans, the Spaniards were first introduced to the difficulties associated with living with people of different beliefs. This was further intensified and worsened under the Visigoth kings. From the Visigoths, the Spaniards learned the profitability of money and laws, and how to utilize both to makes themselves achieve their desires. However, under the Muslims, all of these came together to create the framework and outline of the culture that followed Spaniards into the modern-day. It was during the time of the Muslims that the Spaniards molded and adapted their language, culture, and very identity based upon their close proximity and relations with people of other religions. Had the Spaniards been able to develop into a nation like the other European nations, history itself may have come out differently. However, that is a study for another time.

Statement of Problem

Is there some way to look at the history of Spain that can shed new light on the idea of tolerance in Medieval Spain? The problem with most studies of tolerance in Medieval Spain is that they are often exclusively from the perspective that there was either complete tolerance or little-to-no tolerance at all in Medieval Spain. The historians that are famous for their beliefs of near complete tolerance are the historians Americo Castro, Chris Lowney, and Maria Rosa Menocal, most notably. In their books they go into great detail about the very intricate ways in which Christians, Muslims, and Jews were tolerant of each other and adapted their identity to be able to coexist among people of other faiths. However, the historians Jane S. Gerber, Henry Charles Lea, and John Powers focus on the various negative and highly intolerant actions of life in Medieval Spain. However, these perspectives are not showing the more realistic, and often more complicated picture, in which Medieval Spain was minimally tolerant, among a highly restrictive and controlling world. Historians who get the closest to holding this opinion are the historians Joseph F. O'Callaghan and Raymond Carr. These men emphasize the more realistic view that both the intolerant and the tolerant can exist in the same realm. This unique idea proves that the world of Medieval Spain could be both tolerant and intolerant at the same time.

One of the first weaknesses discovered in the past research is the fact that most of the other scholars of the field merely rush over the idea of money and the value that money had to the kings and emirs of Medieval Spain. With money comes the ability to control the outcomes of various aspects of life. When the Muslims established the city of Cordoba, it became the central hub of intellectual and cultural exchange. More than that, the Muslim rulers with a simple tax would allow the subjects of their rule to worship their religion without persecution. Most historians focus on the wrong aspect of this ruling. They are focusing on the fact that people were able to worship as they wanted. However, it is actually the fact that many of these Christians and Jews under Muslim rule, and later Muslims and Jews under Christian rule, were paying rather large tributes in order to worship the way that they wanted. It is rather tolerant of the leaders of the government to do that, but actually they are manipulating the system in order to gain a large revenue from the people underneath them. Therefore, one can see how that action would explain how there was tolerance in Medieval Spain, but at the same time, the tolerance was not out of genuine acceptance, but out of greed and desire to increase the power of the governments. Further research into this aspect of Medieval Spain will hopefully give more of an understanding that the finances and profits that the Muslim emirs and Christian kings gained from tributes had more significance than formerly thought.

Another weakness in the research is under the aspect of laws, regulations, and religious ideology. Most of the research shows historians merely using these laws to point out the tolerant laws or the intolerant laws. There is more to these laws than historians are examining. For example, an important Muslim religious code states that the Muslim must respect the "people of the book." According to sources, the "people of the book" were people of monotheistic faiths that used a book as a pivotal part of their faith. This includes Christians and Jews; therefore, it became even religiously difficult to truly be intolerant toward someone of other faiths. However, there were also many secular laws that also stated various codes of conduct and behavior for citizens of the cities and towns of Medieval Spain. Therefore, especially in Muslim Spain, they were bound religiously and secularly with codes to respect each other. Despite these laws and regulations, violence still spawned out of prejudice and the stress of the three faiths having to live and cohabitate in such close proximity. Regardless, these laws have been in recent centuries used to explain that the nature of Medieval Spain was either highly tolerant or intolerant. A study into greater detail on the various laws codes and fueros of Medieval Spain will reveal the idea that the Christian kings and Muslim emirs were using secular and religious laws to profit from the people.

The final weakness discovered in the research of this era relates to war. It is well understood that there was much intrigue and war among the kings and emirs of Christian and Muslim Spain. However, one difference with this study is the fact that further research in this topic will prove that these wars had great importance in the wars and in-fighting that occurred in Medieval Spain. For example, during the era commonly referred to as the *Reconquista*, Christian Spain started a long systematic effort to take back Spain from the Muslims. Research into this will prove that the kings would then take the lands that were conquered and instantly institute their laws of *tolerance*, which instantly would start to help them fund further re-conquest.

Significance to the Field

While there have been many interesting contributions to the topic of tolerance in Medieval Spain over the past century, this project will contribute many interesting ideas to the field. One of the significant contributions to the field that will come from this study is the fact that it will create a more defined, more complete, less fragmented look into Medieval Spanish history. Before this study, the history of Spain was fragmented focusing on the Inquisition, Muslim Spain, and the *Reconquista* as separate entities. This study will hopefully bring together the topics and create a subfield to Medieval Spain that will analyze the various ways that Spanish history can be combined. Also, another significance to the field coming from this study is the idea that further interest will hopefully be created in the study of Spain, in general. Too many times, when one examines a world history or European history textbook, Spain is often delegated to a short paragraph or sentence. This will hopefully reinvigorate the study of Spanish history. Finally, one can see how the study can be contributed to today's world. In the Middle East, United States, India, and various other countries, there still exists intolerance between religions. It was complicated ever since the attacks on September

11, 2001, but they existed even prior to that. It will hopefully show that without knowledge and understanding of the core tenets of people of other religions and lifestyles, the intolerance will continue.

Limitations

Unfortunately, with any project, there will always be some limitations to the fulfillment of a project. One of the largest limitations to this project was time. While sixteen weeks is a large amount of time to complete a vast array of tasks, some tasks had to be done with less care than others. The researcher still took great care to complete the tasks required, but summaries of books had to be viewed instead of having the pleasure of reading actual sources in full. One of the most daunting limitations was the fact that more time to thoroughly read and intake more sources of information was needed. To alleviate this problem, the researcher did start early, reading several of the required materials and completed the readings in a satisfactory amount of time. Additionally, another limitation that was discovered was the problem of the language barrier. While the researcher had a workable skill in the language of Spanish, the researcher would have loved to read in greater detail more sources from Spanish authors, as well as read more primary sources in Spanish, but the researcher's skill was not completely up to the level needed to perform this aspect of the study. Therefore, the researcher had to rely on mostly sources that were translated and written in English. Furthermore, along those lines, it would have been helpful to truly go to one of the archives in Spain where many of the original primary sources are kept, but time, money, and distance hindered this

aspect of study.

CHAPTER II: LITERATURE REVIEW

How an event of the past is studied is dependent upon a vast array of ways in which the event is recorded by the people who lived it. More than that, history is also dependent upon the personal feelings and intentions of the author of the history. Furthermore, a history can be affected by the surroundings in which the author is living. It is for these reasons that historiography and the literature review are vital and highly important tools for the historian. In the simplest terms, historiography is the history of history. In more complex terms, it is an examination into what authors in the past have said on a specific topic and how they were affected by surroundings within the world of the historian. It is through the examination of these differences that weaknesses can be found in the scholarship of past historians. It is from this point that other historians can exploit the weaknesses and use it to further the specific field of history for other historians. These historiographic examinations often come in the form of literature reviews. This valuable mechanism allows a historian to quickly read what other historians have stated on the subject, without having to dedicate the hours required to read the works of previous authors.

With that in mind, it is now time to present a literature review and historiographic analysis of Spanish history. However, since the purpose of this study is not an in-depth analysis of the complete history of Spain, but an examination of tolerance in Medieval Spain, the sources analyzed will involve sources that discussed tolerance in Medieval

Spain. There will be a brief description of the original sources of Spanish history, but that will be mainly used as a comparison and example on how the ideas of the historians of Spanish history evolved their views over time. Then the review will describe the main aspect of this project, that being the secondary sources of study. The researcher will examine the sources, discuss the claims and points of the authors, but then point out any weaknesses in their arguments, and how they apply to the overall thesis of the researcher.

Literature Review

The history of Spain has not always focused on the aspect of tolerance and peace during Medieval Spain. The majority of the early histories of Spain were not analysis into tolerance, but encyclopedic recollections of history from the limits of recollection to the current time of the historian. One of the first prominent historians of medieval Spain was Isidore of Seville. Isidore of Seville wrote his histories during the time of Visigoth rule.[41] A unique aspect of Isidore's view on history is the fact that Isidore believed that the Visigoths were chosen by God to conquer Hispania.[42] Therefore, much of the writings of Isidore state that Spain is a divinely ordained place, and that its people can do nothing wrong.[43] As historian Gifford Davis describes, one can see the sprouting of the idea of "patriotism" from the writings of Isidore.[44] Gifford also describes the writing of

---

[41] Alex Novikoff, "Between Tolerance and Intolerance in Medieval Spain: An Historiographic Enigma," *Medieval Encounters* 11, no. 1-2 (November 24, 2005), 11.

[42] Ibid.

[43] Ibid.

Isidore as "[h]e speaks neither of the people, nor of a common past, nor of future goals, but very fulsomely of a land blest by indulgent nature with all advantages of climate, vegetation, animal life, and mineral wealth, a land which the Goths took for their own and where they dwell in secure felicity."[45] From this, one can see that Gifford is proving the claim that Isidore was writing of a land blessed by God. Although his writing was not highly accepted until the thirteenth century, Lucas de Tuy wrote a history of Spain commissioned by Doña Berenguela.[46] However, as was the tradition of the time, there was not much new information added, and Lucas de Tuy "…merely drew on his predecessors, piecing together their annals and adding his own contribution to bring the whole up to date."[47] While he may have imitated the styles of his historical predecessors, he did contribute certain aspects of the history of Spain that was different from those before him. This aspect was the idea of nationality, the idea of being a unique people.[48] One would see this idea of nationality re-emerge with the beginning of the *Reconquista*.

The historical literature of the *Reconquista* is a unique blending of Christian, Muslim, and Jewish sources. One *Reconquista* author was Jose Antonio Conde, and his

---

[44] Gifford Davis, "The Development of National Theme in Medieval Castilian Literature," *Hispanic Review* 3, no. 2 (April 1935), 149.

[45] Ibid.

[46] Ibid., 150.

[47] Ibid.

[48] Ibid.

unique contribution to Spanish history was his use of Arabic writings.[49] Unlike the

historians before him, he was writing the history of the Arabs in Spain.[50] It was Conde

who established the Muslim invasion as 711 and the conquest of Granada in 1492.[51] The

fifteenth and sixteenth centuries saw the rise of histories that started to attribute blame on

certain peoples. For example, historian Don Franzisco de Quevedo blamed the French

and the Germans, and Conde blamed the Muslims for the rise in intolerance and

prejudice.[52]

It was during the nineteenth and twentieth centuries when the history of Spain

started to turn away from mere annals and historians and started to analyze various

unique ideas associated with Spanish history. Francisco Javier Simonet was the first

historian to propose the idea that the Muslims had no influence on medieval Christian

culture.[53] Instead Simonet over-emphasized the accomplishments of Christian Spain, and

he also glorified the martyrdom of the Christians under Muslim rule, mozarabs.[54] Adolfo

de Castro was the first historian to bring the plight of the Jews in Medieval Spain into the

_____

[49] Novikoff, 12.

[50] Ibid.

[51] Ibid.

[52] Ibid., 12-13.

[53] Ibid., 14.

[54] Ibid.

public eye.[55] This is a vital step in the historiography of Medieval Spain because by this point a history of the Christian, Muslim, and Jew was available for public consumption. Furthermore, it was Castro that began the discussion of tolerance, even though at the time he was not aware of the fact. He spoke of the fact that the Jews experienced periods of intermittent oppression and persecution, while at other times the Jews were accepted.[56] From this point forward, tolerance slowly appears into public discussion. Jose Amador de los Rios is noted for his observation that tolerance changed to intolerance under Alfonso VIII and Ferdinand III.[57] De los Rios is also popular for his observation that the peace that other historians were beginning to claim was exaggerated, and not realistic.[58]

In the late nineteenth century and early twentieth century, Henry Charles Lea added to the historiography of Medieval Spain the idea of Inquisition as the end of any last remnant of tolerance and peace between Christians, Muslims, and Jews.[59] For example, in an article from 1896, Henry Charles Lea states,

> The terrible massacres of the Jews, in 1391, form a turning point in
> Spanish history. They mark the end of the ages of toleration, during
> which the peninsula afforded a refuge to the unfortunate children of Israel,

---

[55] Ibid.

[56] Ibid., 15.

[57] Ibid.

[58] Ibid.

[59] Ibid., 16.

and the commencement of the fierce spirit of persecution which rendered the Inquisition inevitable, which expelled the Jews and Moors, and which, by insisting on the absolute uniformity of belief, condemned Spain to the intellectual and material lethargy that marked its period of decadence.[60]

From the work of Henry Charles Lea, historians gained the idea of the division of tolerance into early tolerance, followed by a period of persecution.[61] Essentially, Lea was stating that tolerance existed, but institutions like the Inquisition were catastrophic for the fragile balance of toleration.

In the early years of the twentieth century, historians started to find interest in understanding the relations between the various religious groups, and how each affected one another. Julian Ribera examined the impact of Arabic on medieval Spanish culture.[62] Also, Miguel Asin Palacios analyzed the impact of Islam on medieval Christian theology.[63] One of the more important historians of the early twentieth century was Ramon Menendez Pidal. He is famous for his large works of translation and studies on Spanish identity and language.[64] Because of him, historians have a much larger collection of primary sources at their disposal. Otherwise, historians would have had to translate many

---

[60] Henry Charles Lea, "Ferrand Martinez and the Massacres of 1391," *American Historical Review* 1, no. 2 (1896), 209, in Alex Novikoff, "Between Tolerance and Intolerance in Medieval Spain: A Historiographic Enigma," *Medieval Encounters* 11, 1-2 (November 24, 2005), 16-17.

[61] Novikoff, 17.

[62] Ibid., 18.

[63] Ibid.

[64] Ibid.

more sources from the Castilian to English.[65] It was the work of these men that eventually set up the great debate between Americo Castro and Claudio Sanchez-Albronoz.

The debate started in 1948 when Americo Castro wrote a book entitled *España en su historia: cristianos, moros, y judios*.[66] The book has since been translated several times and has become a staple for any historian of Spain. What is so interesting about this text is that it drastically changed the way that many historians saw the history of Spain, and it gained attention from other historians, such as Claudio Sanchez-Albornoz. In Castro's book he states that the Spanish only became true Spaniards during the years of Muslim occupation; therefore, the Spaniards were affected by the coexistence with Muslims.[67] Furthermore, in the writings of Castro, he states the fact that tolerance existed because "…religious tolerance and the harmonious life together with Mohammedanism and other faiths facilitated the exploitation of the conquered countries, and offered the Moslem the possibility of expanding his interests in the changing aspects of life from the Euphrates to the Ebro."[68] This greatly agitated the fellow historian

---

[65] Ibid.

[66] Ibid., 20.

[67] Ibid.

[68] Americo Castro, *The Spaniards: An Introduction to Their History*, in Alex Novikoff, "Between Tolerance and Intolerance in Medieval Spain: An Historiographic Enigma," *Medieval Encounters* 11, no. 1-2 (November 24, 2005): 21.

Claudio Sanchez-Albornoz, and he fired back with a two-volume discussion on the idea,

where he states the following:

> …the exalted vital passion and the ardent religious enthusiasm do not go
> well with the practice of tolerance. To triumph over the foolish inclination
> of man to suppress the adversary, tolerance requires a singular
> temperamental coldness, coolness in faith, or a great reasoning capacity,
> and an integral culture…Medieval-Hispano-Christian tolerance? Yes, but
> tolerance of the minorities, not of the people, moved by passion and
> inflamed with fervor for the divine war. Popular intolerance grew as the
> people, not finding bellicose or colonizing channels for the venting of their
> impetus for action, looked to domestic life and clashed both with the
> aristocracy, who indulged in the political power from the Trastamaras, and
> with the jews who, protected by the kings and the nobilities, possessed
> wealth and the most lucrative professions.[69]

Essentially, Sanchez-Albronoz is stating that tolerance was perhaps between

fellow Christians, but to think that the minorities were accepted is foolish. This debate

went on for decades, and no scholar to date has successfully found a logical and complete

explanation of what form of tolerance truly existed in Medieval Spain. However, that is

one of the problems in the arguments of the previous historians. They have all been

attempting to explain whether there was complete tolerance, or no tolerance. Castro

claims that the close proximity between the different religions was an aspect of political

desire. However, he never really expands on that point. Sanchez-Albornoz, however,

states that tolerance was mostly between the other Christians, but not so much between

---

[69] Claudio Sanchez-Albornoz, "Spain, a Historical Enigma," in Alex Novikoff, "Between
Tolerance and Intolerance in Medieval Spain: A Historiographical Enigma," *Medieval Encounters* 11, no.
1-2 (November 24, 2005), 23.

Christians and the minorities. This in essence is true. Tolerance, or an acceptance of another's views and beliefs, did not happen. However, due to legal requirements and the various other reasons to be discussed later, it appeared to the people of the time and to historians like Castro that tolerance did exist. They were merely focusing on the acceptance of language, dress, and culture, and not focusing on how this mirage of tolerance was being created.

The first historian to try to blend the two ideas did not come along until the 1980s, and his name was Thomas Glick. He is famous for his attempt to blend ideas together, and through this he has made major headway into the idea of tolerance in Medieval Spain. One of his central arguments is the discussion of acculturation versus assimilation. Essentially, his central argument states that "…it is perfectly conceivable that hostilities between Muslims and Christians over the centuries were accompanied by the eventual Christian adoption of Muslim diet, agricultural techniques, technology, urban institutions, economic life, and even language."[70] This is a very plausible and solid argument. It is proven that with the close proximity between the three religions certain aspects of each other were adopted by those available. However, that does not explain the way that historians are still under the impression that this acceptance of the lifestyle was out of a utopian coexistence among the Christians, Muslims, and Jews. This project

---

[70] Novikoff, 29.

will prove that in fact the true tolerance was a side-effect of the manipulations of government, money, and war to create the image that tolerance existed.

One historian of the twenty-first century that has gotten a great deal of attention for her work on the history of Medieval Spain is the historian Maria Rosa Menocal. In her book *The Ornament of the World: How Muslims, Jews, and Christians Created a Culture of Tolerance in Medieval Spain,* Menocal spends a large majority of the book focusing on the cultural and social acceptance and toleration between the three religions. She presents valid claims and uses the same sources as many historians before her. Yet her central argument is that in the early years of Medieval Spain there was complete tolerance and peace in the realms of Muslim Spain.[71] However, due to the confusion of other Muslim sects, segregation, plague, and the intolerance of Ferdinand and Isabella, tolerance disappeared and ceased to exist in Medieval Spain.[72] While these are interesting ideas, they are not correct. She focuses on the cultural and social tolerance as *the reason* for tolerance, but she does not stop to consider the laws put in place and how they worked to control people.

Through examination of this literature review, one should be able to see that the solution to the problem is rather simple. Historians since the dawn of Medieval Spanish

---

[71] Maria Rosa Menocal, *The Ornament of the World: How Muslims, Jews, and Christians Created a Culture of Tolerance in Medieval Spain,* (New York: Back Bay Books, 2002), 266.

[72] Ibid., 267-271.

historiography have been writing on the history of Spain as if there were separate parts. They either write on the Muslim view of Spain, the Jewish view of Spain, or the Christian view on Spain. That is the first problem. There needs to be a combination of the ideas, and the view of Medieval Spain needs to be viewed from the perspective of them all being Spaniards regardless of religious affiliation. Another problem is the fact that they are all looking at the aspect of tolerance as either tolerant or intolerant. That also needs to be changed. Tolerance existed, but nowhere near the idea viewed by historians like Menocal. The idea of tolerance needs to be thought of as a side-effect, and not a reason. The main focus of future research needs to focus on the idea that Medieval Spain was a peninsula occupied with people of at least three religious viewpoints. Therefore, due to Muslim ideology of acceptance of the "people of the book" and due to Christian ideas of "love your neighbor," they were religiously obligated to at least be civil toward each other.

CHAPTER III: LAWS OF TOLERANCE

In Medieval Spain there was a mirage of tolerance that existed, and that is why, for the better part of a century, historians have been debating over to what degree tolerance existed in Medieval Spain. One source of evidence that historians have used during this time has been the use of a vast array of laws and regulations that the Christian kings and Muslim emirs utilized out of acceptance and tolerance of people of other faiths. These laws were both repressive and fair, and they molded the very fabric of the behavior of the inhabitants of Medieval Spain. However, this is, in fact, an incomplete evaluation of the sources. Historians have not really examined the place that the religious tenets played in forming this mirage of tolerance. Through the evaluation of the religious sources, it will become clear that the Christians, Muslims, and Jews were each following their own religion, which all have elements that preach of acceptance. Furthermore, through the evaluation of the secular laws, one will see that the kings and emirs were using the already existing religious ideology to strengthen the control over the public. This then causes the illusion that people are living in a world of false tolerance, in which every person loves and accepts each other. Unfortunately, this is overly optimistic and too utopian to be considered a rational description of the situation in Medieval Spain. How could tolerance, in the idea of complete acceptance, exist if there were still wars between Christians, Muslims, and Jews? This will also prove to be highly beneficial to the kings and emirs. Through the thorough examination of the religious and secular sources, it will become apparent that these laws created an environment where Christian, Muslim, and Jewish citizens had to be tolerant.

Religious Law

In this period of history, religious life was very important. It was not only important to the individual, but it was also a weapon to be used against others of different religious beliefs. Religion, of course, was one of the many reasons behind the Crusades in the eleventh century. However, in Medieval Spain, religion played a pivotal part in the history of the area. After the conquest of Spain by the Muslims in 711, Muslims pushed the Christian kings to the north, and the Muslims controlled approximately seventy-five percent of Spain. Furthermore, under the Muslims in Al-Andalusia, as they called Spain, there were many Christians and Jews living under these Muslims. They were faced with the difficult job of living among each other. Considering the clash of languages, cultures, and identities, the Muslims and Christians used other terms to describe the Christians, Muslims, and Jews. For example, a *Mozarab* was someone who still retained their Christian faith, but still lived under the Muslim rule.[73] Likewise, a *Mudejar* was a Muslim who still retained their beliefs, but lived under Christian rule.[74]

Legally, whether it was a Christian king or a Muslim emir, Christians, Muslims, and Jews were allowed to keep their religious beliefs as long as they paid a tax sometimes

---

[73] Constable, 564.

[74] Ibid.

called a *jizya*.[75] These *jizya* funded the government, and it allowed the Christians, Muslims, and Jews to worship as they saw fit. This is the concept that historians of the past have often used to explain the idea of tolerance in Medieval Spain. However, these secular laws were not the only laws that molded the behavior of the citizens of Medieval Spain. It was, in fact, the basic tenet of their religions that had a profound contribution to how they behaved. The Bible preaches the idea of acceptance of neighbors, the Quran has a very unique idea of tolerance of the "people of the book", and the Torah uses the Ten Commandments for a medium for their treatment of other people. Therefore, it is vital to the understanding of tolerance to take a closer look at how these religious texts formed the bedrock of what is often perceived as tolerance in the eyes of historians.

The Quran is believed to be the words of the Prophet Muhammed, spoken to him by Allah. Muslims claim that Allah is the Arabic word for God, and that the God of the Christians and Jews is also the God of the Muslims. The Muslims are also associated with the Christians and the Jews because they are believed to be also Abrahamic religions. In other words, all three religions are closely tied together in many ways. That is why Muslims often refer to Christians and Jews as "people of the book". The Arabic word for this idea is *dhimmi*, and it is understood as meaning any Christian or Jew who lives under the rule of the Muslims.[76]

---

[75] Ibid., 563.
[76] Constable, 562.

The idea of acceptance and *toleration* of Christians and Jews was a requirement for their religious beliefs. There are several statements in the Quran that can back up this idea. One excerpt from the Quran states,

> O People of the Book! come to common terms as between us and you: that we worship none but Allah; that we associate no partners with Him; that we erect not from among ourselves Lords and patrons other than Allah."[77]

In this excerpt, the Quran is stating that the "people of the book" need to see each other on the same level and not be prejudiced against each other because they all believe in God. This is interesting because it shows that at the most basic level Muslims were required by their religion to tolerate the Jews and the Christians. Therefore, out of the desire to worship the way that they wanted to, the Muslims were tolerant of the Christians and the Jews. Furthermore, the Quran also states, "Abraham was not a Jew nor yet a Christian but he was true in faith and bowed his will to Allah's (which is Islam) and he joined not gods with Allah."[78] This is another sign from the Quran that it does not matter who the person is; as long as they believe in Allah, and have no other gods, the person can live a great life. This is another sign that an idea of equality was present in these ideas from the Quran. Therefore, when the Christians, Muslims, and Jews were acting in a tolerant fashion, they were following this ideology.

---

[77] Quran 3:64.

[78] Ibid., 68.

Like the Quran, the Bible also has its set religious laws that Christians are to follow. That one idea can be found in Mark 12:31, where Mark states, "And the second, like it, is this: 'You shall love your neighbor as yourself.' There is no other commandment greater…"[79] This, in addition to the Ten Commandments, were the main principles of religious law that the Christians followed. It formed their behavior, and through these laws they acted upon these laws. Therefore, when the scripture says for them to love everyone, they were religiously compelled. Therefore, when they lived alongside the Muslims and Jews, they tolerated them, not because they fully accepted their beliefs, but in that most basic level felt that their specific interpretation of religious thought obligated them to do it.

Furthermore, the Jews were not without their laws that they had to follow. The Jewish Torah is essentially the first five books of the Christian Old Testament. Therefore, many of the religious laws that the Jews followed were based upon the teachings in the Torah. Therefore, this controlled how the Jews behaved around people of other faiths.

However, the researcher is not under the impression that all citizens of Medieval Spain were devout Christians, Muslims, or Jews. Obviously, this would be difficult to prove. Just like today, there are people who are not devout, but the same principle still stands. The Christians, Muslims, and Jews were descended from people who had grown

_____

[79] Mark 12:31.

up with the same ideas and principles, and it was molded into their very character.

Therefore, the Christians were raised to believe that loving one's neighbor was the proper

thing to do. Christians (devout or not) would still try to treat everyone with respect.

Muslims would have been taught that the Muslims were superior, but they were to

respect the "people of the book" not so much out of appreciation but out of sympathy.

They would have seen the Christians and the Jews as close to viewing religion the proper

way, but just short of the goal. In fact, according to a source translated into English from

Arabic by Thomas E. Burnam, a Mozarab states that Christianity is an imperfect Islam.[80]

It would be the similarities in their religions that would have definitely made it possible

to have a degree of respect for people of different religions, but it was not perfect.

Religious prejudices still prospered despite these basic religious tenets molding their

behavior. However, it was the secular laws of the land that helped to further control the

people. Essentially, the religious laws are based on respect, and not full acceptance and

tolerance.

---

[80] Ahmad ibn 'Abd al-Samad al-Khazraji, edited by 'Abd al-Majid al-Sharfi, translated by Thomas E. Burman, "Maqami al-Sulban," in *Medieval Iberia: Readings from Christian, Muslim, and Jewish Sources,* edited by Olivia Remie Constable, Second Edition, (Philadelphia, PA: University of Pennsylvania Press, 2012), 190-194; Ahmad Hijazi al-Saqqa, ed, translated by Thomas E. Burman, "Al-I'lam bi-ma fi din al-nasara min al-fasad wa-awham wa-izhar mahasin din al-islam wa-ithbat nubuwwat nabiyina Muhammad 'alayhi al-salat wa-al-salams," in *Medieval Iberia: Readings from Christian, Muslim, and Jewish Sources*, edited by Olivia Remie Constable, Second Edition, (Philadelphia, PA: University of Pennsylvania Press, 2012), 194-198.

Secular

The religious laws were important to understand because they helped to clarify the concept that at the base of it all, the people were drawn to the respect of people of other religious beliefs due to the fact that their religions specifically require the believer to do so. However, in addition to this level of law, there is also the laws of the land, or the secular laws. The secular laws were introduced to the people in a large variety of forms. There were the *fueros*, law codes, charters, and statutes, to name a few. Through the examination of these sources, and what they say specifically in regards to tolerance, one will see that tolerance was not out of the genuine desire of the people, but because the government saw it as the best way to control and profit from the people.

General Laws

When it comes to general laws and regulations of Medieval Spain, the most important and most often spoken about concept was that of the *jizya*. As defined earlier by Arthur Goldschmidt, Jr. and Lawrence Davidson, the *jizya* was a "[p]er capita tax formerly paid by non-Muslim males living under Muslim law."[81] This tax was put in place throughout Muslim Spain. The *jizya* was a way to appear tolerant to the Christian and Jewish citizens of Muslim Spain. The law allowed anyone who paid this tax to worship their religion without interference. This idea was used by Christian kings as well, but it was not referred to as a *jizya*, but a tax or tribute. Whether it was in Christian

---

[81] Goldshmidt, Jr. and Davidson, 470.

48

Spain or Muslim Spain, this idea of freedom to worship with a payment was an important key to this mirage of tolerance. An example of the rules that were given to the citizens of the cities and towns of Medieval Spain can be found in the *Pact of 'Umar.* This source is an agreement between the Umayyad caliph 'Umar and his Syrian Christian subjects.[82] The pact is written to 'Umar, and it is from the perspective of the Christian subjects.[83] The source opens, "When you came against us, we asked you for safe-conduct for ourselves, our descendants, our property, and the people of our community, and we undertook the following obligations toward you."[84] From this it becomes obvious that tolerance was not wanted, but a necessity out of the fear that their lives and families would be ruined. Therefore, these Syrian Christians conceded to the idea of being subjects to a Muslim leader and took the pact. From the source one learns that the citizens vowed to not build churches, be kind and courteous to Muslims, not convert anyone to Christianity, not sell alcohol, and not display crosses.[85] These are the rights that the Christians gave up when they agreed to submit to the Muslim leaders. However, if one were to look at the source again, they would see that there is more in these words than is often discussed. If one looks at these sources with the opinion that the

---

[82] Constable, 43.

[83] Ibid.

[84] Bernard Lewis, ed. and trans, "Islam from the Prophet Muhammad to the Capture of Constantinople," In *Medieval Iberia: Readings from Christian, Muslim, and Jewish Sources*, edited by Olivia Remie Constable, Second Edition, (Philadelphia, PA: University Of Pennsylvania Press, 2012), 43.

[85] Ibid., 43-44.

government was preoccupied with the idea of control, this changes from a repressive law code into a law that was created to make it easier for the government to control the people. For example, the decision to not build churches or display crosses was actually a way of keeping violence to a minimum. If Christians were allowed to openly build churches, display crosses, and attempt to convert people to Christianity, it would have created problems. With the implementation of this rule, it made any incidents of these events the problem of the Christian, and not the king or emir because he had warned the people.

The same idea can also be seen in what is commonly referred to as the "Treaty of Tudmir." In this document one can learn many things. The first thing that is inherently obvious is the fact that it is an inversion of the *Pact of 'Umar*. Therefore, this source records the institution of tolerant laws from Muslim subjects to a Christian king.[86] The treaty states,

> We ['Abd al-Aziz] will not set special conditions for him or any among his men, nor harass him, nor remove him from power. His followers will not be killed or taken prisoner, nor will they be separated from their women or children. They will not be coerced in matters of religion, their churches will not be burned, nor will sacred objects be taken from the realm, [so long as] he [Tudmir] remains sincere....[87]

---

[86] Al-Dabbi, edited by Francisco Codera and Julian Ribera, translated by Olivia Remie Constable, "Kitab bughyat al-multamis fi ta'rikh rijal ahl al-Andalus," in *Medieval Iberia: Readings from Christian, Muslim, and Jewish Sources*, edited by Olivia Remie Constable, second edition (Philadelphia, PA: University of Pennsylvania Press, 2012), 45-46.

[87] Ibid., 259.

Once again in this document one can see that the Muslims will be allowed to keep their religious beliefs, as long as the leader of the Muslim people submits to the power of the Christian king. Furthermore, lands and possessions of the people will be left untouched, and the people can continue living their lives. However, once again, one can see that Tudmir merely wanted the land that was occupied and, instead of going through a long costly battle, saw it as simpler to gain this land through the idea of tolerance and acceptance. Furthermore, it becomes apparent that this was also another strategy to prevent chaos and riots.

If one follows this string of thought, it becomes apparent that the regulation of the markets and bazaars in the plazas was of similar intention. From a twelfth century source called the *Hisba* Manual, Bernard Lewis has translated the source for easier examination. This source is essentially a list of rules that a *muhtasib* must follow to regulate the selling and buying of items in the bazaars and markets.[88] One observation that has been made in the past is the fact that the major cities were the intellectual centers of exchange, and that tolerance existed there. However, with so many people in one area, to have any event of intolerance and violence could cause riots, the number one enemy of many kingdoms and empires. Therefore, the regulations of the markets were vital. The layout of where

---

[88] A muhtasib was an individual who was in charge of making sure that the daily sells in the market ran smoothly. Ibn 'Abdun, Translated by Bernard Lewis, "Islam from the Prophet Muhammad to the Capture of Constantinople," in *Medieval Iberia: Readings from Christian, Muslim, and Jewish Sources*, edited by Olivia Remie Constable, Second Edition, (Philadelphia, PA: University of Pennsylvania Press, 2012), 227-231.

Muslims, Christians, and Jews could place their merchandise and where they could not was an important job. For example, Muslims view their mosque as a place of purity and worship; therefore, one of the first rules for the *muhtasib* was, "[t]here must be no sellers of olive oil around the mosque, nor of dirty products, nor of anything from which an irremovable stain can be feared."[89] Furthermore, the *Hisba* Manual also states that nothing dead should be placed near the mosque, but that is once again out of sanitation purposes, and not out of intolerance to the person selling the items.[90] With the closeness of the markets, it would have been difficult to not have interaction between Christians, Muslims, and Jews. In the text of the *Hisba* Manual, there are certain aspects that seem intolerant or prejudiced against Christians and Jews. Even if the chance occurred that a Muslim did become friends with the Christian or Jew, they would still have to follow these rules. The rules of regulation for the markets were strict and semi-intolerant out of the desire to prevent any riots or violent actions to occur in the market. If a violent event like that would occur, it would be bad for the image of the government. A government should be able to control its citizens, and a government that cannot is a weak government.

Fueros

 Fueros and statutes are also important sources of information in regards to the question of tolerance in Medieval Spain. Like the general laws, these laws were

---

[89] Ibid., 227.

[90] Ibid.

instituted to control the various aspects of life in Medieval Spain, which included the relationship between Christians, Muslims, and Jews. Through the examination of these sources, it will become apparent that the fueros, charters, and statutes were more methods of control over the lives of Christians, Muslims, and Jews in Medieval Spain.

The *Fuero Juzgo* was written during the period of time when the Visigoths controlled Spain.[91] One defining feature of Visigoth Spain was that they were highly anti-Semitic in their beliefs. Therefore, it is rather understandable that many of the laws found in the *Fuero Juzgo* can be considered pre-cursor ideas to the Inquisition.[92] However, most of the *fueros* were not overly repressive and were antiquated and old fashioned even then when it was written, considering the many references to Roman and Christian laws that can be discovered in its pages.[93]

However, another fuero, the *Fuero of Teruel,* was written in 1176 and was more prejudiced in nature of both Muslim and Jew. This massive fuero was written by Alfonso II of Aragon , and it contains many laws in regards to the relationship between Christians, Muslims and Jews. Many of the selected laws discuss how Christians, Muslims, and Jews were to be represented in the court setting.. One law that can be considered tolerant

---

[91] Wm. T. Strong, "The Fueros of Northern Spain," *Political Science Quarterly* 8, no. 2 (June 1893): 320, accessed October 13, 2015, http://www.jstor.org/stable/2139647.

[92] Ibid.

[93] Ibid.

is the law that states that judges must "…appoint public brokers…to sell things…. The sellers and the brokers shall swear that they will be honest in all things, alike for poor as for rich, whether they be Christians or Jews or even Moors."[94] This appears tolerant because it was a mechanism to guarantee that regardless of religion or financial status, the broker and sellers were going to be fair in the marketplace. Like the market regulations discussed before, the judges were making the brokers make these vows in order to make the brokers and sellers liable if a riot broke out between the Christians, Muslims, and Jews over unfair selling practices. This law was obviously put into place to guarantee that relations between the people of different religions would be hospitable, and it would cut down on violence. There are also various laws regarding how the Jews and Christians would be represented in courts of law, when Jews, Christians, and Muslims could go to the bath houses, and how much in fines they would have to pay if they overlapped, or disregarded the rules.[95] From these rules many concepts become apparent. First of all, there was a structure and order in the cities, towns, and villages of Medieval Spain. Despite living in such close proximity, there was a large degree of segregation in the cities. For example, Muslims and Jews could only go to the public baths on Fridays, while Christian males were allowed to go on "…Tuesdays and Thursdays and Saturdays…."[96] This was established to control the interaction between

---

[94] Elka Klein, trans., "El Fuero de Teruel," *Medieval Sourcebook,* accessed October 9, 2015, http://legacy.gordham.edu/halsall/source/1276teruel.asp.

[95] Ibid.

the citizens, and once again to reduce the chances of violence. In many ways, it has become apparent that the governments were using these tolerant actions to not so much be tolerant, but because they wanted to prevent enemies from seeing them as weak because they could not adequately control their kingdom. In regards to the laws on how Christians, Muslims, and Jews were to be represented in court, this is perhaps a law of genuine tolerance. To give each religion representation in the Teruel government shows that they did not want to lord over their citizens with dictator-like qualities.

Perhaps one of the most popular *fueros* for historians to examine is that of the *Fuero de Cuenca*. This law code of 1177 deals primarily with the many facets of organizing the land and the people.[97] This *fuero* was written roughly around the same time as the previous *fuero*, the *Fuero of Teruel.*[98] This law code has the generic information regarding who is responsible of owning palaces, who has authority of the children, and how to prosecute a bigamist, but this *fuero* has many laws in regards to the relationship between Christians, Muslims, and Jews.[99] One of the first laws is the standard law of anyone who comes to live in Cuenca will have the freedom to worship as

---

[96] Ibid.

[97] Constable, 221.

[98] Ibid.

[99] James F. Powers, ed. and trans., "The Code of Cuenca: Municipal Law in the Twelfth-Century," in *Medieval Iberia: Readings from Christian, Muslim, and Jewish Sources,* edited by Olivia Remie Constable, second edition (Philadelphia, PA: University of Pennsylvania Press, 2012), 221-224.

they please, as long as they pay the tribute.[100] This law became more prevalent as the era

of the *Reconquista* became stronger. As the Christians started to conquer more and more

land from the Muslims, the Christian kings saw it beneficial financially and morally to

allow the citizens to stay. If the king were to send the citizens away, the kingdom would

lose large amounts of money, and it would put Spain in danger of reprisals from their

enemies. Another interesting law from the *Fuero de Cuenca* is in regards to children

born out of relations between a Muslim woman and a Christian man.[101] It states, "If

anyone has a child with another's Moorish woman, this child should be the servant of the

señor of the Moorish woman, until his father redeems him. Also, we say that such a child

should not divide with his siblings that which correspondence to the patrimony of their

father, while he remains in servitude. Later should he become free, he would take a share

of the goods of his father."[102] This is important because while technically relations

between the religions were forbidden, they did occur. Therefore, the governments had to

find ways to handle such situations. Therefore, that is why this one rule was put into

place. Even though the government could say that those born of this union are worthless,

they did in fact give them the chance to get a measure of equality among the other

citizens of Medieval Spain. The next law can be read as extremely prejudiced and

---

[100] Ibid., 221-222.

[101] Ibid., 223.

[102] Ibid.

negative. It states, "Whoever sells or gives weapons or food to the Muslims let him be hurled from the city cliffs, if it can be proved; but if not, he should clear himself with twelve citizens and should be believed…"[103] Upon first glance, this appears to be perhaps one of the most intolerant laws. While it is harsh, one should also notice the clause where the law states that they do have a chance to redeem themselves before a jury of twelve fellow citizens. Therefore, it is in the most limited way generous toward the citizen. In regards to tolerance, this law was the government's way to conserve food for its citizens. According to *The Medieval Sourcebook* around the time the *Fuero de Cuenca* was written, the population of Spain/Portugal would have been roughly between seven and nine million.[104] The cities of Medieval Spain were large and making food go around to all of its citizens was hard. Therefore, to give away food could have been seen as sinful, and therefore, the government put forth this strict law.

Law Codes

In addition to the general laws and *fueros,* there were the law codes that were in some capacity written by the kings of Spain.[105] The most famous law codes include the *Lex Visigothorum, Las Siete Partidas,* and the *Usatges of Barcelona.* There are also

---

[103] Ibid.

[104] Josiah C. Russel, "Tables on Population in Medieval Europe," *Medieval Sourcebook,* accessed October 5, 2015, http://legacy.fordham.edu/halsall/source/pop-in-eur.asp.

[105] From the research conducted, it appears that the majority of the major law codes were written by Christian kings. It appears that the Muslim leaders relied mostly on the general laws and *fueros* to control society.

various other ruling statutes that were decided on during the Third and Sixth Councils of Toledo. Through the analysis of these sources, it will become apparent that the true intentions of the Christian kings was the control of the populous, which caused the mirage of tolerance that has become so prevalent in the scholarship of Medieval Spain.

One of the first major law codes of Spain was written during the waning years of the Visigoth control of Spain. This document was the *Lex Visigothorum*. In this document, there are many laws indicating the rule of the land, but there is also a great deal of information regarding how the Jewish people were to be represented in court.[106] In this law code one can learn the fact that Jews were forbidden the right to testify against Christians.[107] This could mean many things. It could be a mechanism to prevent chaos, but the most likely reason was the fact that Christians were seen as superior to other religions; therefore, it was a mechanism to preserve the appearance of the Christian. A society that was truly tolerant would not have a legislation like this. They would allow all parties of different religions to represent themselves. Therefore, one can say that the people of the seventh century were not completely tolerant of the Jews, but they accepted them as sources of income. This law also has an exception, which is rather dubious. It states that any Jew that is "found acceptable" was allowed a small measure of

[106] Karl Zeumer, ed., translated by Jeremy duQ. Adams, "Monumenta Germaniae Historica: Legum sectio I, Leges Visigothorum;" Jacob R. Marcus, ed. and trans, "Monumenta Germaniae Historica: XII, 2, 17;" Jacob R. Marcus, ed. and trans, "Monumenta Germaniae Historica: XII, 3, 3," in *Medieval Iberia: Readings from Christian, Muslim and Jewish Sources*, edited by Olivia Remie Constable, (Philadelphia, PA: University of Pennsylvania Press, 2012), 23-26.

[107] Zeumer, 24.

representation.[108] However, this is saying that the Jew would have to behave in a way that is not Jewish to be considered "acceptable". Another common practice of the era was to attempt to convert Jews to Christianity. These converted Jews were often required to follow strict rules to retain the status as a converted Jew. Therefore, the *Lex Visigothorum* has information on how those Jews were supposed to behave. Some of these rules include,

> …we will observe no Jewish customs or rites whatever, and will not associate or have any intercourse with any unbaptized Jews. Nor will we marry any person related to us by blood, with the sixth degree, which union has been declared to be incestuous and wicked.[109]

The law then goes on to list the various Jewish holidays that they would no longer follow. The law stated that they accept the punishment of relapsing into Judaism which was "…he shall be burned, or stoned to death…."[110] This last law is rather important. It points out that the Jew was made accountable for their own failure to strictly abide by the Christian faith. Therefore, if they did not follow the religion of Christianity, they knew that a horrible death sentence was in store for them. Once again a tolerant nation would not have forcefully made people worship a specific religion. They would have accepted the individual for who they were, regardless of religion. However, this did not occur.

---

[108] Ibid.

[109] Marcus, 24.

[110] Ibid., 24-26.

Another major law code that was written during the era of Medieval Spain was

the *Usatges of Barcelona*. This document was written as the basis for a constitution for

the city of Barcelona, and it like the rest of the laws has many interesting laws regarding

the relationship between Christians, Muslims, and Jews. One of the most interesting

points made in the *Usatges* is the fact of the description of *how* a ruler should appear to

his people. This law plainly states the following claim on behavior of the king.

> Since a land and its inhabitants are ruined for all time by an evil prince who is without
> truth and justice, therefore, we the oft-mentioned princes…decree and command that all
> princes who will succeed us in this princely office shall have a sincere and perfect faith
> and truthful speech for all men, noble and ignoble, kings and princes, magnates and
> knights…Christians and Saracens, Jews and heretics, might trust and believe in the
> princes without any fear or evil suspicion for their persons but also for their cities and
> castles, fiefs and property, wives and children, and for anything they possess…And
> among other matters, let the peace and promise not take violent action which the princes
> should give to Spain and the Saracens on land and sea be maintained by them.[111]

From this excerpt, one can plainly see that the government of Barcelona was concerned

with how their leaders were perceived. This can also be seen in *Las Siete Partidas* (to be

discussed in detail later), in regards to how a king should be seen by the public. It can be

learned from *Las Siete Partidas* that a king should have the following qualities: "perform

his actions with a good demeanor…dress with great elegance…be gentle…eager to learn

to read…be dexterous…[and] be skillful in hunting…."[112] One can see that it was vital

---

[111] Joan Bastardis I Parera, ed., translated by Donald Kagay, "Usatges de Barcelona: El codi a mitjan segle XIII," in *Medieval Iberia: Readings from Christian, Muslim, and Jewish Sources*, edited by Olivia Remie Constable, Second edition, (Philadelphia, PA: University of Pennsylvania Press, 2012), 166.

[112] Samuel Parsons Scott, ed. and trans., "*Las Siete Partidas*," in *Medieval Iberia: Readings from Christian, Muslim, and Jewish Sources*, edited by Olivia Remie Constable, second edition (Philadelphia, PA: University of Pennsylvania Press, 2012), 377-382.

for the king to keep up certain images, otherwise his authority could be questioned.

Therefore, it was important for them to create an environment where everything appeared as if life was tolerant. This can be seen by his statement "…let the peace and promise not take violent action which the princes should give to Spain and the Saracens on land and sea be maintained by them."[113] This point is further strengthened by the statement from the excerpt which states that the Christians, Jews, and Muslims were to trust and believe in the kings and princes of Spain.[114] Another interesting law that can be found in the *Usatges* is the law which reads, "[l]et Jews swear to Christians but Christian never swear to them [Jews]."[115] This is a rather interesting law, but it has many interesting meanings. This law shows that the Christians had no problem being sworn to (meaning they had no problem being in control over a Jew) but they did not like the idea of a Jew ruling or controlling a Christian. It is apparent that a truly tolerant nation would not have such a law. This proves that the Christians of Muslim Spain also viewed Jews as inferior. There is also an interesting law which states that if anyone causes a converted Muslim or Jew to turn away from Christianity, he was to pay a fine of "twenty golden ounces of Valencia…."[116] This is important because during the twelfth and thirteenth century the

[113] Ibid.

[114] Ibid.

[115] Donald Kagay, ed. and trans, *The Usatges of Barcelona: The Fundamental Law of Catalonia*, (Philadelphia, PA: University of Pennsylvania Press, 1994) accessed October 14, 2015, http://library.uca.edu/usatges/opening.htm.

[116] Ibid.

Reconquista was active, and the goal was to make Spain Christian again, and if the converts were swayed away, it would be counter-productive. There is also a law that states that a Christian is not to sell any weapons to a Muslim.[117] This rule was put in place to attempt to guarantee that violence and actions of prejudice did not occur.

Perhaps one of the greatest historical legal documents in the history of Medieval Spain, *Las Siete Partidas,* has been used for decades for the examination of the history of Spain. This document which was written in the early fourteenth century was used for many reasons. Historians in the past have used this document to analyze its descriptions of the relationship between the Christians, Muslims, and Jews.[118] It is also a large source of information of the place a slave held in Medieval Spain.[119] An analysis of these sources will give a greater understanding to the argument that the laws were used to benefit the government, and creation of a mirage of a tolerance was a way to succeed at this mission.

Slavery existed in Medieval Spain. Unlike the slavery of America, this slavery was not primarily based on race. However, there was a larger portion of slaves that were of Muslim and Jewish ethnicity in Medieval Spain. That is why there is a section of *Las*

---

[117] Ibid.

[118] Scott, 399-405.

[119] Ibid., 393-398.

Siete Partidas that discusses slavery. It is also of great importance to the argument at hand regarding tolerance in Medieval Spain. The author of *Las Siete Partidas* defines slavery as "…men who are under obligation to those to whom they belong…."[120] It has often been stated that the kings of Spain considered the Jews to be slaves of Spain forever. Therefore, they were bound to Spain as a source of income. Furthermore, *Las Siete Partidas* explains that no Christian can be a slave to a Jew or a Muslim.[121] This is all about superiority over those that the government viewed as inferior. The kings of Spain at this time were starting to gain more strength, authority, and land over the Muslims, and this gave them the confidence to start making such claims of the inferiority of the Muslims and the Jews. This put a great stress on the relations of the Muslims and Jews living under Christian kings. Tolerance, as has been described by previous historians, is not prevalent in these situations. A tolerant society would truly not see other peoples as inferior. A truly tolerant nation would see all people as equal.

Another major aspect of the laws in *Las Siete Partidas* is the aspect of the legal status of the Jews and the Muslims. This law code specifically outlines various ideas, including how the Jews and Muslims should behave in the presence of Christians, penalties for Christians who become Jewish, how to recognize a Jew, and how to punish those who insult converts.[122] One interesting law describes how Jews should behave

---

[120] Ibid., 393.

[121] Ibid., 396.

around Christians. This law is restrictive because it retards any true qualities of Jewishness to a level that the Christians could handle.[123] It states, "Jews should pass their lives among Christians quietly and without disorder, practicing their own religious rites, and not speaking ill of the faith of Our Lord Jesus Christ, which Christians acknowledge."[124] This law is repressive for two reasons. It prevents the Jews from truly practicing their religion and causes them to merely exist to serve the king and benefit him. The law then goes on to state that any individual who refuses to follow the law properly will be put to death and their property will be claimed by the government.[125] This leads into the money aspect of the mirage of tolerance that was being created by the government of Spain. However, for now it should be satisfactory to say that the tributes from the *jizya* were no longer "paying the bills," and Spain needed new methods to collect and gain money from its subjects.

To counterbalance the previous negative law, another law was more lenient and respectful of the Jewish people. There is a law in *Las Siete Partidas* that states that Jews are not allowed to build *new* synagogues in the city of Castile, but they can rebuild any that are damaged or destroyed.[126] There is even a provision in the law that states that no

---

[122] Ibid., 399-403.

[123] Ibid., 399.

[124] Ibid.

[125] Ibid.

[126] Ibid., 400.

64

Christian is allowed to damage or deface the synagogue in anyway, and anyone that does damage it will be strongly fined.[127] This is one of the few signs of genuine tolerance and compromise found in the history of Medieval Spain. The government did not want any synagogues being built bigger or better than a Christian church, but they were tolerant enough to allow Jews to still have somewhere to worship. From reading this law, one can immediately see that in this law code there are many contradictions. That is one reason that historians for centuries have been debating over whether Spain was truly tolerant. One law is tolerant and the next one could be intolerant. Therefore, when a historian is examining these sources, they must examine the motives and intentions of each individual law. Taking these two laws as an example, the answer can be summarized as manipulation. The first law discussed stated that Jews were forbidden to disrupt the public peace by agitating people and worshipping in public.[128] However, the next law discussed stated that they could build churches that were destroyed in some form, and Christians were forbidden from defacing them.[129] Separately these two laws are contradictory, but once evaluated together for what they truly are they make sense. The government was using the Jews of Spain. Instead of the government having to pay to rebuild a synagogue, the government put the Jews in charge of rebuilding the synagogue.

---

[127] Ibid.

[128] Ibid., 399.

[129] Ibid., 400.

This way it both preserved the image of tolerance, at the same time preventing any kind of major altercations or riots. Adding in the provision stating that Christians were not allowed to damage the synagogue can be seen as further manipulation of the fear the Jews had of damages to their already fragile life under Christian rule.

Another law that is found in *Las Siete Partidas* is the law concerning how to discern and pick out a Jew from a crowd. This law states that a Jew should "...bear certain marks in order that they may be known."[130] This law states very plainly the intentions of the government in regards to the reasoning behind such a law. The law states the following information.

> Many crimes and outrageous things occur between Christians and Jews because they live together in cities, and dress alike; and in order to avoid the offenses and evils which take place for this reason, We deem it proper, and we order that all Jews, male and female, living in our dominions shall bear some distinguishing mark upon their heads so that people may plainly recognize a Jew, or a Jewess, and any Jew who does not bear such a mark, shall pay for each time he is found without it ten maravedis of gold....[131]

It can be plainly seen from this excerpt that the government was preoccupied with their appearance, but also with the desire to prevent any violent or prejudice actions in their cities. Therefore, they felt it was only logical and reasonable to install this law that makes the Jew more obvious to the Christians. However, it is also important to discuss the fact that the author pointed out to the reader that aspects of *true tolerance* were taking

---

[130] Scott, 402; Jacob Marcus, *The Jew in the Medieval World: A Sourcebook, 315-1791*, (New York: JPS, 1938), 34-42.

[131] Ibid.

place in the fact that Jews were beginning to dress like Christians.[132] This shows that there was definitely a degree of adoption of culture and styles of dress as part of the association with the people of other religions.

However, Jews were not the only people in Medieval Spain with the Christians. There were also the Muslims, and there are also many rules that are discussed in *Las Siete Partidas*. The idea of tolerance should be replaced with more of an idea of compromise. This can be seen in the statement in *Las Siete Partidas* which states, "We decree that Moors shall live among Christians in the same way that we mentioned in the proceeding Title that Jews shall do, by observing their own law and not insulting ours."[133] From this statement, one can see that the government was accepting the fact that they understood that they had to live by each other.

Up to this point much of the discussion has been an in-depth examination of the various laws of tolerance and intolerance that were recorded in the various forms of religious and secular laws of Medieval Spain. Yet, now it is vital to discuss in further detail how these laws were used to create the image of tolerance in Medieval Spain through the use of the idea of control. Through legal and religious control the government limited the lifestyles and ability to openly express views. The Christians,

---

[132] Ibid.

[133] Robert I Burns, ed., *Middle Ages Series: Las Siete Partidas,* (Philadelphia, Pennsylvania Press, 2000), 1438; Scott, 403.

Muslims, and Jews were living in close proximity to each other, and they understood that this made life difficult on the cultures of all involved. The entire issue has nothing to do with whether the Christians, Muslims, and Jews loved or hated each other. Joseph F. O'Callaghan explains, they were merely three religious groups trying to live "within certain limits to practice their religion and be governed by their own laws and by their own judges."[134] Thomas F. Glick and Oriol Pi-Sunyer further describe this situation when they state "[g]iven the need of two or more cultures to operate in a pluralistic setting, protracted contact tends to result in mutual agreements, recognized ground rules, for stabilized cultural relations."[135] Essentially, Glick and Pi-Sunyer are stating that it was inevitable that these three cultures would present some form of tolerance to those studying the situation. However, it was not out of personal acceptance and tolerance as historians like Maria Rosa Menocal present, but more along the lines that they understand societal norms required them to exhibit some co-habitational mechanisms to handle each other. That one method of making it possible to live among each other with a modicum of civility is the use of laws and restrictions. It may appear repressive and cruel that the governments were restricting the expression of its Christian, Muslim, or Jewish citizens, but these governments were trying to prevent disaster. However, this restriction in

---

[134] O'Callaghan, 23.

[135] Thomas F. Glick and Oriol Pi-Sunyer, "Acculturation as an Explanatory Concept in Spanish History," *Comparative Studies in Society and History* 11, no. 2 (April 1969): 140-141, accessed August 11, 2015, http://www.jstor.org/stable/178249.

essence created one of the few mediums of true tolerance of the era, which was the poetry of the era. Glick and Pi-Sunyer also present the evidence that describes another form of true tolerance. They state, that with the Christians, Muslims, and Jews living in such close proximity, it is inevitable that they naturally started to assimilate and mold certain habits, such as dress and language.[136] However, the restrictive laws of the government prevented Christians, Jews, and Muslims from truly living up to their religious identities due to the fact that they had fear of offending and inciting riot among the other religious groups. The laws of Medieval Spain were, in essence, a model of behavior that all citizens of both Muslim, and Christian Spain were required to obey. O'Callaghan once again states here plainly that each religious group came to Spain with their own unique cultural norms, or as he claims, "…the chief source of law was custom, unwritten law sanctioned by usage from time immemorial."[137] Therefore, much of the behavioral models that the three religious groups followed was based on laws and rules that they had been following for centuries. When a person of one religious belief behaved in a way that was seen offensive to the person of another religion, this caused problems. Therefore, it was a necessity to make laws that create an environment where everyone is equal, and no one person is superior to the other. This was done, unfortunately, by

---

[136] Ibid., 141.

[137] O'Callaghan, 171.

instituting laws that also appear intolerant and harsh to people of the time and to

historians today.

CHAPTER IV: MONEY AND TOLERANCE

More influential to the mirage of tolerance than the place of laws in controlling the people, money was another pivotal concept in creating the illusion of tolerance in Medieval Spain. In fact, money and how to obtain vast amounts of it was the main focus of many of the endeavors of the government and was the motivation behind many of the laws put into place to control the people. These ideas can be further realized through the examination of the *Jizya* and other various forms of tribute in Medieval Spain. As previously discussed, the *Jizya* was a tax that required religious minorities to pay a tax to be allowed to worship as they desired and to be free of any kind of persecution for their beliefs. Therefore, under Christian rule, the Muslims and the Jews paid this tax, and under the Muslims, the Jews and the Christians paid the tax. This tax has created the mirage that Medieval Spain was tolerant of people of Christian, Muslim, or Jewish belief. Yet, in all actuality, this was a period of exploitation and manipulation of a population of peoples merely trying to coexist. One should consider the revenue that the governments of Muslim and Christian Spain gained from these tributes. While it was not a huge portion of their income, it would have certainly allowed the governments to continue the tax as long as possible. However, this was not the only form of tribute that was collected from the citizens that can be seen as *tolerant*. There were also tributes paid as part of pacts and treaties to be discussed later. However, once Christian Spain began the period

of the *Reconquista*, the idea of the tributes for freedom of religion was beginning to

slowly wane. Therefore, when King Ferdinand and Queen Isabella instituted the

Inquisition in 1478, not only did the mirage of tolerance dissolve, but also it was utilized

as a mechanism of persecution and profit from those accused. Therefore, through the

examination of tributes, inquisitorial records, and descriptions of the *Reconquista*, it will

become apparent that money played a pivotal part in the creation and destruction of the

mirage of tolerance.

Jizya and Tributes

One way that the government of Medieval Spain made money was through the

use of tributes. A tribute can be anything from taxes paid from a conquered city or town

for protection by the government, a tax as a part of a pact or treaty, or it could be like the

jizya, which was used as a method of allowing the subjects to worship their own specific

religion without prejudice. Whatever form this tribute came in, it was a form of income

to both Muslim and Christian Spain. One problem with the tribute is the fact that there

was not a set standard price. The governments of the cities could implement any price

they thought effective to run their governments. This can be seen in *The Book of*

Tradition, which describes the actions of a Jewish Administrator under Caliph Hisham.[138]

This text states that the Jewish administrator could "…adjudicate all their litigations, and

---

[138] Constable., 91-92.

that he was empowered to appoint over them whomsoever he wished and to exact from them any tax or payment to which they might subject."[139] The whole situation was overly unique. Primarily, they have a Jewish official being in charge of setting the taxes. This creates the illusion that the government was tolerant because they were letting a religious minority have a position of power. While this occurred, it was not overly common and often incited violence. However, this could also be seen as a way of placing the blame on the Jewish administrator if he places the tax rate too high. In relation to the situation with this specific Jewish administrator, he was eventually thrown in prison for taking money from the public.[140]

Another problem that was often seen in regards to the tributes was that the tributes were often set at a price much larger than people could afford, to further take advantage of the situation. According to *The Tibyan*, 'Abd Allah ibn Buluggin states that Alfonso "…describe[s] and justif[ies] his actions as ruler of Granada in a time of political difficulty."[141] One excerpt from *The Tibyan* describes 'Abd Allah ibn Buluggin's frustration over the prices of the *jizya*.

---

[139] Abraham ibn Daud, edited and translated by Gerson D. Cohen, "The Book of Tradition," in *Medieval Iberia: Readings from Christian, Muslim, and Jewish Sources,* edited by Olivia Remie Constable, second edition (Philadelphia, PA: University of Pennsylvania Press, 2012), 92.

[140] Ibid.

[141] Constable, 142.

I argued the matter with Álvar Háeñez and said I could not afford to pay him [Alfonso] anything. I gave the Almoravids as an excuse and pleaded other expenses which I had to spend on them. The swine made no comment and, bound as he was to serve his master...loyally, he sent a messenger to him with a request that he send an envoy to me to demand his tribute. If the envoy returned empty-handed, Álvar Háeñez would retaliate by attacking my territories.[142]

Later in *The Tibyan,* 'Abd Allah ibn Buluggin states that he is accused of owing three years of tributes amounting to over 30,000 *mithqals.*[143] Despite the fact that this was the price for the entire city of Granada, it is amazing to assume a single city could afford to pay such an amount. More than that, it is amazing to see that Christian Spain and Muslim Spain were profiting greatly from this tax on tolerance. However, to the benefit of the Spanish government, certain kings and queens discovered this practice and instituted certain rulings preventing people in charge of taxation from putting in place extraordinary taxes.[144]

War was a common occurrence throughout Medieval Spain. However, the payment of tributes to the victor of a battle was often a way of securing land. Therefore, that was another way that Christians and Muslim Spain gained income from their

---

[142] 'Abd Allah ibn Buluggin, edited and translated by Amin T. Tibi, "Tibyan," in *Medieval Iberia: Readings from Christian, Muslim, and Jewish Sources,* edited by Olivia Remie Constable, second edition (Philadelphia, PA: University of Pennsylvania Press, 2012), 144.

[143] Of interesting note, in modern United States dollars, 30,000 mithqal would amount to $3,795,600, according to http://glossary.bahaiq.com/pages/mithqal. That is an astronomical amount to have to pay in a three year period. That works out to roughly $1, 265, 200 a year.

[144] Joseph O'Callaghan, ed. and trans., "Cortes de los antiguas reinos de Leon y de Castilla," in *Medieval Iberia: Readings from Christian, Muslim, and Jewish Sources,* edited by Olivia Remie Constable, second edition, (Philadelphia, PA: University of Pennsylvania Press, 2012), 350.

victories was through the exploitation of these tributes paid by the vanquished. This can be seen as described in the chronicle of the King Sancho I of Aragon found in the *Chronicle of San Juan de la Peña.*[145] In this chronicle the author explained that King Sancho had such a strong control over the city of Huesca, that the Muslims paid him tribute, but doubled the tribute if King Alfonso and his army would take control over King Sancho's piece of Spain.[146] The role this played in regards to war will be discussed in the next chapter. Alfonso accepted the plea because they are promised double the tribute. Therefore, in the end Alfonso's kingdom comes out looking more tolerant and more powerful. It was an easy decision for King Alfonso.

Money was a very central aspect of the power of Christian and Muslim Spain. Both the Christians and the Muslims created opulent and majestic cities in Medieval Spain, each with huge centers of learning and cultural exchange, more so in Muslim Spain. However, the only way to retain these cities such as Cordoba, a city of magnificent prestige and beauty, was to have a constant supply of money to pay for the up-keep of maintenance and production. Therefore, it was important that the people of Spain contributed many forms of income to the government. While the following documents do not deal specifically with tolerance, they did contribute to the idea that

---

[145] Constable, 157.

[146] Lynn H. Nelson, ed. and trans, "The Chronicle of San Juan de la Peña," in *Medieval Iberia: Readings from Christian, Muslim, and Jewish Sources,* edited by Olivia Remie Constable, second edition (Philadelphia, PA: University of Pennsylvania Press, 2012), 160.

Spain was more interested in the profit of the economy than in the welfare and true relationships between its citizens. Therefore, one can look at the documents from the city of Vic which describe various ways in which its citizens gave up certain freedoms to landlords for the chance to merely live on a patch of land.[147] For example, in "Vic, Arxiu Capitular, calaix 6, 2213, 27 April 1101," a man named Arbert Salamó was to give "3 quarters of feed-grain and 3 hens to Ramon Bermund...."[148] Bermund was the owner of the land, and, out of permission to live on the land, Bermund required the grain and hens as a "tribute" price. The same thing can be said from the sources "Vic, Arxiu Capitular, Liber dotationum antiquarum, folio 146v, 18 March 1212" and "Vic, Arxiu Capitiular, calaix 7, 223, 23 December 1269", where the leaders of the land required some form of payment as a means to secure the men's right to live on a certain land.[149] This shows in some aspects, regardless of religion, people were being taken advantage of for money, land, or possessions.

One can also see the manipulation of the government system when one examines the court documents from the era. In a court document from Barcelona concerning a

---

[147] Paul Freedman, ed. and trans, "Vic Arxiu Capitular, calaix 6, 2213, 27 April 1101," "Vic, Arxiu capitular, Liber dotationum antiquarum, folio 146v, 18 March 1212," Vic, Arxiu Capitular, calaix 7, 223, 23 December 1269," in *Medieval Iberia: Readings from Christian, Muslim, and Jewish Sources,* edited by Olivia Remie Constable, second edition, (Philadelphia, PA: University of Pennsylvania Press, 2012), 311-313.

[148] "Vic, Arxiu Capitular, calaix 6, 2213, 27 April 1101," 312.

[149] :"Vic, Arxiu Capitular, Liber dotationum antiquarum, folio 146v, 18 March 1212;" "Vic, Arxiu Capitular, calaix 7, 223, 23 December 1269," 312-313.

Jewish widow and her daughter, one can see that not only prejudice existed, but also the desire for money and excess was present. In the document, a Jewish mother was widowed and was having trouble taking care of her daughter, as well as having trouble keeping up with the property that her husband left her.[150] In that specific court case, the woman's land is sold for a small amount of money.[151] However, the Jewish woman loses her property because she has nothing else of value, and the court does not want to pay her out of some other fund. Therefore, the Jewish woman is not only treated in an intolerant way, but she is also left homeless and with only a small inheritance to pay for a new piece of land.

Proof that can be seen for the outrage of how Spain was obsessed with money is from the words of people who lived during that time. There were men of the era who were not fooled by the false illusions of tolerance that the governments were creating. It can be found in the writings of Juan Ruíz in his *Libro de buen amor*. In this text, Ruíz speaks of the corruption and evil that money brings.[152] Some of the most profound statements include some of the following excerpts.

---

[150] Elka Klein, ed. and trans., Arxiu Capitular de Barcelona, in *Medieval Iberia: Readings from Christian, Muslim, and Jewish Sources*, edited by Olivia Remie Constable, second edition, (Philadelphia, PA: University of Pennsylvania Press, 2012), 339-342.

[151] Ibid.

[152] Constable, 421.

Money works miracles and is to be greatly cherished for it makes the man of slow wit respectable and competent. It makes the lame run and the dumb speak and the man without hands eager to grasp it....

In the Roman Court where His Holiness resides, I saw that everyone present did obeisance to money. They all honored it with due solemnity and bowed down before it as if to His Majesty....

I saw wonders worked where it has held in abundance. Many deserved to die and it gave them life; others were innocent and it had them killed; it caused the loss of many souls and was the salvation of many others....

It makes the poor man lose his house, vineyards, furniture and all his roots, casting everything into disarray. The whole world is plagued by its curse and where money prevails many things are overlooked....[153]

Ruíz was trying to make the point that money is both something important, but also a curse on humanity. Through the use of money, wonderful things can be achieved, but it is also the medium through which many truly terrible things have been perpetrated. Therefore, when it comes to money, one must use money responsibly, otherwise one's life can be ruined. In this text, Ruíz also relays the idea that even the mighty church can be perverted by the use of money and the desire for more.[154] Therefore, it can be seen from the examination of the tributes and other taxes of Medieval Spain that Spain was greedy and often used any method available to gain more money for Christian or Muslim Spain. However, this was not the only method that Christian and Muslim Spain used to take advantage of the Christians, Muslims, and Jews living in Medieval Spain. There was also the utilization of the *Reconquista* to profit from the manipulation of people.

---

[153] Juan Ruíz, edited by G. B. Gybbon-Moneypenny, translated by Jill R. Webster, "Libro de buen amor," in *Medieval Iberia: Readings from Christian, Muslim, and Jewish Sources,* edited by Olivia Remie Constable, second edition, (Philadelphia, PA: University of Pennsylvania Press, 2012), 421-422.

[154] Ibid.

Reconquista

The *Reconquista* was another aspect of the history of Medieval Spain that utilized the desire for money to create the illusion that people were being tolerant. It was during the *Reconquista* that Christian Spain started to gain power and quickly gain back lands that had been under Muslim control for centuries. However, once the lands were reconquered by the Christians, they were faced with the problem of how to repopulate the areas and how to profit from them. One of the first ways they did this was by using the existing laws and regulations to set up control over the cities. These laws made it appear to the conquered that they were being treated fairly, and they could escape persecution. However, they also used various financial and economic means to financially profit from the *Reconquista*. As more lands were conquered, there were more Christians in Spain, but more Jews and Muslims were at the mercy of the Christians. This would have greatly benefitted the finances of the growing Christian state because it would have swelled the funds from the *jizya* to huge proportions. Through resettlement and reorganization of Medieval Spain, Spain once again further added to the self-perpetuation of the mirage of tolerance.

In the early days of the *Reconquista*, Christian kings started to slowly venture farther into Muslim lands and take possession of the lands through military or diplomatic means. However, after the land was reconquered, the king faced the difficulty in reorganizing and resettling the lands. An eleventh century account of how Alfonso VI of

Leon-Castile reorganized the reconquered lands is a great example. One concept that is immediately evident in this account is that it is from the Christian perspective.[155] Therefore, the author portrays the Muslims under the King Yahia Alcadirbille as being mistreated and tortured by their evil Muslim king.[156] This trick makes it look like the Christian king is a caring and compassionate leader, once again perpetuating the mirage of tolerance. More than that, upon taking control of the city of Toledo, King Alfonso VI sets about reorganizing the city.[157] Once again the literature is written in a way that it was for the benefit of the people of the city, and how King Alfonso VI was the caring leader of a persecuted people.[158] Another interesting account discusses how originally upon the re-conquest of Toledo, a mosque was to be kept the way it was out of the great care the king took in the happiness of his subjects. However, the mosque eventually became a Christian church.[159] The one controversial issue discussed in this account is the fact that supposedly the Muslims did not get mad because they knew the king was a tolerant man, and would have not done so without good intentions.[160] There is some

[155] Ramon Menendez Pidal, ed., translated by John Moscatiello, "Primera cronica general de España," in *Medieval Iberia: Readings from Christian, Muslim, and Jewish Sources,* edited by Olivia Remie Constable, second edition, (Philadelphia, PA: University of Pennsylvania Press, 2012), 131-132.

[156] Ibid.

[157] Ibid., 133.

[158] Ibid.

[159] Colin Smith, ed. and trans., "Christians and Moors in Spain," in *Medieval Iberia: Readings from Christian, Muslim, and Jewish Sources,* edited by Olivia Remie Constable, (Philadelphia, PA: University of Pennsylvania Press, 2012), 134-136.

[160] Ibid.

speculation among scholars of the era that the Queen and an archbishop gave permission to the builders to transform the mosque into a church while the king was gone. However, nothing like that would have happened without the king's permission. Therefore, the king, continually interested in appearances, went back on his promise, but blamed it on others to keep up with the mirage of himself as a tolerant leader.

Another example of the manipulation of the image of tolerance can be found in the *Book of Deeds*. This document was supposedly written by King Jaume I of Aragon, but that is difficult to prove.[161] Upon taking over Valencia in the thirteenth century, King Jaume I set about reorganizing the city. His first initiative was to bring Christians into the city and allow Muslims to either leave or live under his rule as loyal subjects.[162] The account then goes on to discuss the point that, with several Muslims leaving the city, many of their possessions that they could not take with them were left unattended and vulnerable to be stolen.[163] Therefore, there were men put in charge of protecting the possessions of those Muslims who left.[164] However, that was merely an action to prevent the average citizen from gaining possessions of the rich Muslims in the city of Valencia.

---

[161] Constable, 273.

[162] Damian J. Smith and Helena Buffery, eds. and trans., "The Book of Deeds," in *Medieval Iberia: Readings from Christian, Muslim, and Jewish Sources,* edited by Olivia Remie Constable, (Philadelphia, PA: University of Pennsylvania Press, 2012), 273.

[163] Ibid., 277.

[164] Ibid.

The author of the *Book of Deeds* then goes on to state that "…we entered the town. And when the third day came we began to divide the houses with the archbishop of Narbonne, the bishops and the nobles who had been with us, and with the knights who had been given inheritances in that district."[165] The *Book of Deeds* then goes into brief detail describing to where the various portions of the lands conquered and taken over were divided.[166] From examining this source, one can see plainly that this was not a true tolerant action, but just the manipulation of the feelings of those involved in the situation. Three days later, the military and the church started going through the possessions and using them for financial gain. It can be seen in the very surrender agreement signed by the leader of Valencia that all Muslims and their "moveable" possessions would be able to leave without objection.[167] The words written down were not to be completely trusted.

It can be seen through the examination of these sources that the kingdoms of Spain were solely interested in money and continually glorifying their benevolence. Therefore, in the sources we can see kings that portrayed their enemies as horrible, evil individuals to make it appear that they themselves were tolerant and caring leaders. In many ways, this act of demonizing the other is a political strategy used throughout the world today. Furthermore, the kings falsely used tolerant legislation to convince

---

[165] Ibid., 277-278.

[166] Ibid., 278.

[167] Robert I. Burns, ed., and trans., "Archive of the Crown of Aragon, Barcelona, Cancilleria Real, Pergaminos de Jaume I, 734," in *Medieval Iberia: Readings from Christian, Muslim, and Jewish Sources,* edited by Olivia Remie Constable, (Philadelphia, PA: University of Pennsylvania Press, 2012), 279.

Muslims to leave their lands, only to claim the possessions for their own three days later. It becomes apparent that promises of tolerance were not hard-set because kings like King Alfonso VI neglected his promise to the Muslims of his city and turned the mosque into a church. These kings were exploiting the people with false tolerance to increase bank accounts and strengthen the image of the Christian kingdom. This approach was further strengthened and used during the Inquisition.

Inquisition

Before the late fourteenth and early fifteenth centuries, Spain had been content with the revenues coming in from using the laws to profit from the people of Spain. However, in the late fourteenth and early fifteenth centuries, the kingdom of Spain saw that they were no longer able to fund their ever-growing endeavors; therefore, the kingdoms needed something to compensate this need. This compensation was found in the Spanish Inquisition. This entity helped to bring in large amounts of revenue; however, it eventually resulted in the disappearance of any veil of tolerance that existed in Medieval Spain and replaced it with fully fledged intolerance and prejudice.

Based on a terrible outbreak of violence in 1390 involving the murder of several Jews, the kingdoms of Spain started to really see the Jewish people as a problem. Therefore, through forced conversions, many Jews were required to convert to Christianity. This event created the caste of Spanish citizens referred to as *conversos*, or Jews or Muslims who converted to Christianity to escape persecution.[168] The creation of the Inquisition was to monitor and judge any *conversos* who strayed from their

conversions.[169] Therefore, at least originally, the main targets of the Inquisition were

conversos, Jews, and Muslims. A truly tolerant nation would not be purposefully

targeting minorities in society. However, this idea is too utopian to be plausible. Due to

the wealth of many of the cities of Spain, some citizens had substantial wealth. Some of

these people were not Christian, but Muslims and Jews. This incited jealousy and

animosity and fueled Inquisition hatred. It is obvious from the writings of the early

Inquisition era that Jews and Muslims were targeted because of their wealth. "Within a

few days three of the most prominent people in the city, and the richest, were burned,

who were Diego de Susán, who they said was worth ten million and a great rabbi…."[170]

The author of this text goes on to explain, "[t]hey seized Pedro Fernandez Benadeba, who

was majordomo of the cathedral…and one of the most prominent men in the cathedral

chapter, and he had in his house enough arms to equip one hundred men…."[171] It is

obvious from this text that the kingdoms of Spain were targeting the wealthy. The

government understood that the Jews and Muslims were becoming financially stable

---

[168] Lu Ann Homza, ed. and trans., *The Spanish Inquisition, 1478-1614: An Anthology of Sources,* (Indianapolis, IN: Hackett Publishing, Inc., 2006), 1-3.

[169] Ibid.

[170] Manuel Gómez-Moreno and Juan de M. Carriazo, "Memorias del reinado de los Reyes catolicos, que escribe el bachiller Andres Bernaldez," in *The Spanish Inquisition, 1478-1614: An Anthology of Sources*, edited and translated by Lu Ann Homza, (Indianapolis, IN: Hackett Publishing, Inc., 2006), 6.

[171] Ibid.

under the illusion of tolerance, and that made them nervous. They saw that they could benefit from having the possessions of these men, including money in weapons. They were not tolerant, but were building up their accounts and stock piles of weapons.

It is also evident from the sources that the men in charge of the Inquisition would come up with any excuse to consider the accused as relapsing into Jewish or Muslim behavior. For example, in the Case of Isabel, wife of bachiller Lope de la Higuera, she was accused of relapsing into her old Jewish ways.[172] Some of the ridiculous accusations made against her were "[s]he does not do any sort of work on Saturday, but instead puts on clean undergarments and clothing, and shaves…and dresses up on these days."[173] Now, it must be understood that according to Jewish tradition, one must not work on Saturday. However, some aspects of Jewish tradition are not necessarily religious in nature, but have become ingrained in the natural habits of the culture. Therefore, when the accuser states that she does not work on Saturday because she is once again practicing Judaism, it is not completely true. However, the action of stating that she needed to be burnt because she changed her undergarments and shaved is totally arbitrary. Later in the case it is announced that, "Isabel, wife of bachiller Lope de la Higuera to be a heretic and apostate. She has incurred a sentence of greater excommunication, and all other spiritual

---

[172] Haim Beinart, "Records of the Trials of the Spanish Inquisition in Ciudad Real," in *The Spanish Inquisition, 1478-1614: An Anthology of Sources*, edited and translated by Lu Ann Homza, (Indianapolis, IN: Hackett Publishing Company, Inc., 2006), 13-16.

[173] Ibid., 15.

and temporal punishments contained in the laws against heretics, as well as the loss and confiscations of her goods."[174] Therefore, she is executed, and all possessions that once belonged to her immediately became the possessions of the kingdom to be used as they saw fit. This is further proof that Spain was not a tolerant nation, but creating a mirage of tolerance to lure unsuspecting prey into their kingdom for exploitation.

A truly tolerant nation would involve someone of the accused religion to defend the individual. However, the judges involved in the Inquisition were not religious judges, but in fact secular.[175] As the historian Henry Charles Lea explains this situation, "[it] was wholly secularized and only to be distinguished from the laity by the sacred functions which rendered its vices most abhorrent by the immunities which fostered and stimulated those vices and by the intolerance which, blind to all aberrations of morals, proclaimed the stake to be the only fitting punishment for aberration in the faith."[176] This gave the kingdom the right to accuse and make up rules to their own benefit. Furthermore, even if a kingdom in Spain did not want to institute the Inquisition, the Catholic Church saw it as vital. Once again, Henry Charles Lea explains that the Church gave so much money to the government of Christian Spain that Christian Spain would do anything that the Church wanted.[177] For example, in a letter to the city of Tarazona, the king ordered those

---

[174] Ibid., 16.

[175] Gomez-Moreno, 6.

[176] Henry Charles Lea, *A History of the Inquisition of Spain*, vol. 1, (Philadelphia, PA, 1905), 11.

[177] Ibid., 12.

in charge to create an Inquisition in that town, or they would obtain a fine of 10,000 gold florins.[178] This shows that certain cities were trying to at least appear tolerant to their Muslim and Jewish citizens, but the kingdoms were requiring the various cities and towns of the kingdom to follow through with the Inquisition.

Discussion

Money is both a blessing and a curse.[179] When it is used properly, it can benefit millions, but when used with the wrong intentions it can condemn the user. In Medieval Spain, the Spanish kingdoms were using money for the purposes of self-promotion. They were using the laws to disguise their actions in a way that made it appear that Medieval Spain had great tolerance. The *jizya* and other forms of tribute were a few of the many sources of income for the kingdoms of Medieval Spain. It was through these tributes that the kingdom was able to continue with the mirage of tolerance that they had created. During this time, the kingdom of Spain was slowly growing in strength because they were re-conquering and reorganizing their lands due to the actions of the *Reconquista*. This not only created more lands, but caused more incentives to utilize the tribute system. Eventually, the tolerance that appeared to exist faded away, and prejudice and intolerance were apparent in full force. That was when the governments of the Spanish kingdoms

---

[178] J. Angel Sesma Muñoz, "El establecimiento de la Inquisicion en Aragon," in *The Spanish Inquisition, 1478-1614: An Anthology of Sources,"* edited by Lu Ann Homza, (Indianapolis, IN: Hackett Publishing Company, Ltd., 2006), 10.

[179] Ruíz, 421-422.

created the Inquisition and used it to compensate for the lack of surpluses of money that they were now losing due to the movement of Muslims and Jews out of highly intolerant areas. Joseph F. O'Callaghan agrees with the fact that the Inquisition was a major mechanism for the gaining of more funds for the Spanish kingdom. To prove this point he quotes a historian of the time, who states,

> All this was done out of a thirst for plunder rather than piety. The people also wanted to do the same to the Moors living in the cities and towns of the kingdom, but they didn't dare to do so, because they were fearful that Christians held captive in Granada or overseas might be killed.[180]

Later in in his book *History of Medieval Spain*, Joseph F. O'Callaghan describes the fact that the exploitation of the Jews and Muslims was the work of the Spanish government.[181] The following excerpt better explains how the government of Spain used the Inquisition to get the money they needed to further continue with their actions of "tolerance."

> All the worst features of the medieval inquisition were to be found in the Spanish Inquisition. It operated secretly; the accused were used to obtain confessions; those convicted were subject to confiscation of property for the benefit of the state, as well as exile, imprisonment, or burning at the stake.[182]

Therefore, with this understood, it becomes apparent that through the manipulation of the laws, control of the people, the use of tributes, the Reconquista, and the Inquisition, the Spanish kingdoms were exploiting the people of Spain. However,

---

[180] Pedro Lopez de Ayala, "Cronica de Enrique," in *A History of Medieval Spain*, edited by Joseph F. O'Callaghan, (New York: Cornell University, 1975), 537.

[181] O'Callaghan, 670.

[182] Ibid., 671.

there is one more mechanism through which the Spaniards exploited the relations

between the citizens. That mechanism was war, and it was found in abundant supply in

Medieval Spain. It was instrumental in the continuation of the mirage of tolerance.

CHAPTER V: WAR AND TOLERANCE

War was a major component to the lives of every citizen of Medieval Spain. This is especially true during the period of the *Reconquista*, in which Christian kingdoms were systematically retaking lands owned by Muslims. However, there was also warfare between Christian kingdoms, and even battles among Muslims, all for the chance at supremacy in Spain. However, it was in this world of wars that the mirage of tolerance was still continued. This can be seen by the various alliances, pacts, and treaties made between Christians and Muslims. There were instances in which Muslim leaders would align with Christian kings in order to defeat an enemy. However, this was not tolerance, but mere military strategy to eliminate or neutralize a common enemy. Furthermore, there was the constant conquest by the Christian kingdoms that was contributing to the increasing Christian kingdom. This correlates with what has already been said regarding the desire for money from the conquered lands, which further helped the continuation of the mirage of tolerance. There were also the various behind the scenes political intentions of the leaders of the governments of Christian and Muslim Spain. All of these ideas come together to show that war was the final part of the tri partite mechanism that allowed for it to appear that tolerance existed in Medieval Spain. Through the examination of these concepts, it will become apparent that war was another means by which Medieval Spain created a mirage of tolerance.

Alliances, Pacts, and Treaties

Alliances, pacts, and treaties were some of the methods that the governments of Spain used to manipulate the mirage of tolerance in Medieval Spain. It was through these alliances, pacts, and treaties that battles were concluded. However, in many of these alliances, pacts, and treaties there were certain accommodations that made the treaties profitable to the winning government. Many of these accommodations were then used to create the appearance that there was tolerance in Medieval Spain. This can be seen through an examination of the sources.

Two pacts that were discussed earlier for their legal importance also hold militaristic importance. Those two sources are "The Pact of 'Umar" and the "Treaty of Tudmir." For example, the "Pact of 'Umar" describes how the conquered Christians would not "…mount on saddles, nor shall we gird swords nor bear any kind of arms nor carry them on our persons."[183] This was obviously a military provision insuring that the conquered people would not rebel, or fear the wrath of the Muslim armies. It allowed the caliph to appear accepting and tolerant. However, it was really a way that the people understood that if they rebelled they would face the wrath of the government that was so generous to give them a tolerant place to live. This idea can also be seen from the "Treaty of Tudmir" where the code essentially states that the leader 'Abd al-Aziz was such a generous person that he would not force any religious ideology upon the

---

[183] Lewis, 44.

conquered people of Tudmir.[184] Instead he would tell the people of Murcia, Orihuela, Valentilla, Alicante, Mula, Bigastro, Ello, and Lorca that they were given religious freedom.[185] What does this show? It shows that tolerance was not only a tool of the legal system, but also the tool of war and conquest. The armies could conquer enemies, and instead of going into battle, they could show "tolerance" and cities would surrender voluntarily. Therefore, this showed a great military strategy on the part of the Muslims because they understood that during the eighth century, during the Muslim conquests, Spain was weak.

These ideas become even more apparent when they are examined from the period of Christian expansion during the *Reconquista*. Under the "Treaty of Cazola" there is evidence that shows that hostility during the period was not always between Muslims and Christians. There was also hostility between Christian kingdoms, and in the case of the "Treaty of Cazola" the hostility was between King Alfonso II of Aragon and Alfonso VIII of Castile.[186] The treaty states that King Alfonso VIII would concede several lands including Valencia to King Alfonso II of Aragon.[187] This is often a source used to argue for/against tolerance in Medieval Spain. One could argue that there *was* tolerance

---

[184] Al-Dabbi, 45.

[185] Ibid.

[186] Constable, 209.

[187] Julio Gonzalez, ed., translated by James W. Brodman, "El reino de Castilla en la epoca de Alfonso VIII," in *Medieval Iberia: Readings from Christian, Muslim, and Jewish Sources,* edited by Olivia Remie Constable, second edition (Philadelphia, PA: University of Pennsylvania Press, 2012), 209-210.

because warfare was rampant during the time, and there was no true motivation to fight Christian or Muslim. However, one could also use that same evidence to argue that tolerance *did not* exist merely for the fact, that if Christian kingdoms could not get along, how could it be expected for Christians to get along with Muslims. However, there were times when Christians did unite against their common Muslim enemy. This can be seen from the examination of an alliance created in the early fourteenth century against the Muslims in Granada. There is an interesting account of the alliances between Aragon and Castile against Granada.[188] In reading the source one can see the various strategies that the Christians kings of Aragon and Castile used to attempt to conquer Granada.[189] This further complicates the image of tolerance in Medieval Spain. However, the argument can be concluded by stating that it was the political intentions of the governments. If it benefited a Christian to align with a Muslim to conquer an opposing Christian, it was done, not out of tolerance, but out of a desire to become the ultimate kingdom and outlast all others.

Sometimes there were more than one version of a treaty. Through analyzing the differences between the treaties, it will become apparent that the many points that each side found as important in the treaty. That can be seen from the examination of the

---

[188] Anna Goodenough, ed. and trans., "The Chronicle of Muntaner," in *Medieval Iberia: Readings from Christian, Muslim, and Jewish Sources,* edited by Olivia Remie Constable, second edition, (Philadelphia, PA: University of Pennsylvania Press, 2012), 303.

[189] Ibid.

"Treaty of al-Azraq." From the Christian perspective of the treaty, one can gain the view that the Christians valued their appearance. It is obvious through the word choice of the treaty that Don Alfonso was to be seen as the benevolent ruler, who though he conquered Abu 'Abd Allah ibn Hudhayl, he was generous to let ibn Hudhayl, "...by the grace of God prince, elder son of the king of Aragon, receive you Abu 'Abd Allah ibn Hudhayl vizier and lord of Alcala as my cherished and much esteemed and very honored and loyal vassal."[190] The treaty then goes on to explain that "[a]nd I grant and give you two castles...."[191] The Christian treaty was using too much pomp and circumstance to make it appear that the two sides were genuinely friendly toward each other. However, this is all part of the mirage. In many ways the Muslim version of the treaty is perhaps the better and more accurate of the treaties. It skips many of the ceremonial salutations and titles and plainly explains how the countryside and possessions were to be separated.[192] In the text, instead of stating that the Christians would give a certain number of castles (because he is a friend), the author of the treaty explains that some castles were to be given up immediately, while others were to be vacated in three years.[193] It is this information that is not given in the Christian treaty, and from that it becomes apparent

---

[190] Robert I. Burns and Paul Chevedden, eds. and trans., "Negotiating Cultures: Bilingual Surrender Treaties in Muslim-Crusader Spain," in *Medieval Iberia: Readings from Christian, Muslim, and Jewish Sources,* edited by Oliva Remie Constable, second edition (Philadelphia, PA: University of Pennsylvania Press, 2012), 284-285.

[191] Ibid., 285.

[192] Ibid.
[193] Ibid.

that the Christians were the prime culprits behind the continuation of the mirage of tolerance.

Conquest

A great deal of information can also be discovered with the analysis of the various descriptions of conquest during Medieval Spain, as to how it relates to the mirage of tolerance. It was through conquest that Muslim Spain gained much of their land during the period of Muslim growth. Muslim Spain controlled nearly seventy-five percent of Spain in the eighth century. Also, it was through conquest and diplomacy that the Christians reconquered much of Spain during the *Reconquista*. Through this period of conquest, both parties used the various methods available to them for the continuation of the mirage of tolerance. Therefore, it is vital to understand what can be gained from these sources.

The first major era of conquest was the conquest of Spain by the Muslims in 711. In this period, there were many mixed emotions regarding how the Muslims would compare in relation to the Visigoth rulers before them. Therefore, it is important to realize that upon initial conquest, many of the people of the peninsula of Spain did not know how to feel. From a contemporary Latin source of that era, one can truly see the prejudice and anger at the conquest of the Muslims. For example, this anonymous author states the following in regards to the conquest of Toledo by a Muslim named Walid. "After forcing his way to Toledo, the royal city, he imposed on the adjacent regions an evil and fraudulent peace."[194] This is perhaps one of the few actual signs that even the

citizens of Spain understood that this peace and tolerance that the leaders were using was

not real. It was merely a mechanism of conquest and acceptance that the militaries used

to soothe the angry conquered peoples and to make them accept their new leaders.

Furthermore, the same author explains how the conquering militaries utilized a tribute

system and used it to add to their own opulence.[195] He stated, "Abd al-'Aziz pacified all

of Spain for three years under the yoke of tribute. After he had taken all the riches and

positions of honor in Seville…."[196] This idea of conquest is painted in a very different

perspective when it is described by a Muslim. From the accounts of Ibn 'Abd al-Hakam

and Ibn al-Qutiyya, they portray the whole situation as if it were an accident.[197] Ibn 'Abd

al-Hakam claims the conquerors were a small reconnaissance force of 1,700 men, and not

a huge army as described by the conquered Christians.[198] Al-Qutiyya's account then

describes the pact that was set up upon Muslim control as a treaty created with honor, the

same one that the anonymous Latin author describes as false.[199] This is one of the many

---

[194] Kenneth B. Wolf, ed. and trans, "Conquerors and Chroniclers of Early Medieval Spain," in *Medieval Iberia: Readings from Christian, Muslim, and Jewish Sources,* edited by Olivia Remie Constable, second edition, (Philadelphia, PA: University of Pennsylvania Press, 2012), 34.

[195] Ibid., 35.

[196] Ibid.

[197] Ibn 'Abd al-Hakam, edited by Charles C. Torrey, translated by David A. Cohen, "Narrative of the Conquest of al-Andalus;" Ibn al-Qutiyya, translated by Ann Christys, "Christians in Al-Andalus, 711-1000," in *Medieval Iberia: Readings from Christian, Muslim, and Jewish Sources,* edited by Olivia Remie Constable, second edition, (Philadelphia, PA: University of Pennsylvania Press, 2012), 36-42.

[198] Al-Hakam, 36.

reasons that historians have trouble deciphering whether there was tolerance in Medieval Spain. They do not know whether to trust the Muslim account that accepts that there was violence, but states that they truly did not intend to conquer approximately seventy-five percent of the Iberian Peninsula. If the Christian perspective is correct, the Muslims were swarming Spain, brutally murdering innocent people, and putting them under control under a false illusion of peace. Since there are so few sources that exist, the historians have to accept many of the sources as having some remnant of truth. From these three sources, one thing can be stated for certain, and that is that war creates chaos and a surge of rhetoric.

Another important conquest of the period of Medieval Spain was the final conquest that changed Spanish history forever, and that was the conquest of Granada in 1492. It was from this conquest that the mirage of tolerance that Muslim and Christian Spain had been trying to continue for so long was destroyed. A contemporary of the event, Hernando del Pulgar chronicles the various events after this conquest.[200] One point that del Pulgar discusses is the fact that thirty days were spent in deliberation after the events of the conquest.[201] This was a rather courteous and gracious undertaking by

---

[199] Wolf, 34; Ibn al-Qutiyya, 42.

[200] Constable, 496.

[201] Hernando del Pulgar, translated by Teofilo Ruiz, "Cronica de los senores reyes catolicos Don Fernando y Dona Isabel," in *Medieval Iberia: Readings from Christian, Muslim, and Jewish Sources*, edited by Olivia Remie Constable, second edition, (Philadelphia, PA: University of Pennsylvania Press, 2012), 496.

the Christian kings. Upon completion of the treaty, the Christian kings made the old

promise that no Muslim would be forced to convert.[202] They also gave the provision in

their treaty that anyone who wanted to leave was welcome to leave, and the only thing

that they would have to leave behind would be weapons.[203] The remainder of the treaty

once again follows the same pattern of discussing clauses that could be taken as actual

tolerant actions. However, upon closer examination, one would be able to see that these

tolerant actions had negative and nefarious intentions. It can be seen in the fake way that

the king worded the various logistics of the treaty. For example, "[a]ll Moors other than

those included in this agreement who desire to enter their highnesses' service within

thirty days may do so and enjoy all the benefits of it...."[204] This is written in a way that

leads the individual to feel that the king is compassionate and accepting of anyone into

the court of the king. However, this was written to deceive the Muslim citizen of Spain

into thinking that they would be welcomed. In reality, the king is covetous of the

possessions of the Muslim people. This can be seen from the next aspect of the treaty

that glorifies the beauty and opulence of the Muslim mosque.[205] Essentially, the king

sees these mosques as a way to continue the mirage of tolerance.

---

[202] Ibid.

[203] L.P. Harvey, ed. and trans., "Islamic Spain, 1250-1500," in *Medieval Iberia: Readings from Christian, Muslim, and Jewish Sources,* edited by Olivia Remie Constable, second edition, (Philadelphia, PA: University of Pennsylvania Press, 2012), 501.

[204] Ibid., 504.

[205] Ibid., 502-503.

Political Intentions

The mirage of tolerance relates to the way in which the kings and leaders of Spain used various aspects of society in Medieval Spain to make it appear that Spain was a tolerant nation. That was to their benefit because it allowed them to extend their nation and become one of the dominant nations in Europe. So far it has been discussed that the various pacts, alliances, and treaties of the era were used to aid in this continuation of the mirage of tolerance. Also, it has been discussed that the conquest as part of expansion was another mechanism in which the government of Medieval Spain used tolerance. As the kings reconquered lands lost to them from the Muslim conquests, they promised those that they conquered the same things that their conquerors promised them, freedom and tolerance.

One of the major political intentions of the governments was the use of alliances, pacts, and treaties as a way to delay warfare until it could be more profitable or more advantageous. This can be seen from many accounts of warfare of Medieval Spain. For example, if one were to look once more at the *Tibyan*, it also has many pieces of evidence that point to governments using warfare and the threats of warfare to get a desired result. For example, Ibn Buluggin states that he asked the Muslim amir Yusuf ibn Tashufin, if they could have reinforcements because they feared an attack from Christians.[206] The amir did not give Ibn Buluggin reinforcements, and the Christians did confront the city.[207]

---

[206] Abd Allah ibn Buluggin, 143.

However, instead of fighting, Tashufin "…concluded a treaty with the prince of Zaragoza and with neighboring princes in the east…who staved off trouble from him by paying him the sums they owed him."[208] The *Tibyan* then further shows the thought process of a leader of the time.

> On receiving this news, I became more anxious than ever and realized that in this business I was like a man on a lion's back. If I surrendered the city…when I had no troops at my disposal, it would be ravaged without my being able to get a single dirham back. Yet I would not be excused, and some schemer would not hesitate to say I had lost it out of carelessness or that I had actually led the enemy into it, just as I had seen and heard the same sort of thing being held against Ibn Rashiq. Moreover, I would have lost my country into the bargain. I would be unable to provide for the annual campaigns we launched against the Christians and for hospitality extended to the Almoravids. My loss would, therefore, be twofold. But if, on the other hand, I sought to placate the enemy and looked to my own interests, it would be said that I had concluded a treaty with the Christian and be discredited for something I had not done, as indeed happened.[209]

From these words of Ibn Buluggin, several concepts are obvious. One idea that is obvious is the fact that leaders were obsessed about his appearance to his people, as well as his appearance to other leaders. Ibn Buluggin is concerned with how he appears to his citizens if he willingly surrenders to the Christians, while at the same time wondering if signing a treaty with the Christians would make him look weak.[210] Ibn Buluggin then finally decides to sign a treaty, and pay a tribute to prevent any Christian or Muslim enemies from entering his realm.[211] What does this say concerning the

---

[207] Ibid.

[208] Ibid.
[209] Ibid., 143.

[210] Ibid.

[211] Ibid.

problem of tolerance in Medieval Spain? This source shows that by postponing warfare or military skirmishing until a later time through the use of a treaty, it allowed the citizens of Aledo to live in their world in which the mirage of tolerance existed. It allowed the mirage to continue.

Discussion

War is a common theme in all aspects of history. However, in Medieval Spain, it was extremely important because of the way it contributed to the mirage of tolerance in Medieval Spain. The Christians, Muslims, and Jews were living alongside each other trying to coexist. The governments of Christian and Muslim Spain were using warfare as one of the mechanisms to control the people. They would use alliances, pacts, and tribute systems to further establish the illusion that they were living a tolerant lifestyle. Christian kings would make alliances with Muslim enemies and fight against common enemies. This is often portrayed as tolerant, but it was not. The Christian king would pair with the Muslim leader because he knew and understood that the Muslim emir had certain beneficial military strategies for the king to come out victorious. These Christians and Muslims were using each other to further and strengthen themselves in a chaotic world. However, they used laws and money they gained from the tributes to continuously implement more "tolerant" laws. The Christian kings and Muslim emirs were using tributes and treaties to delay or stop battles. This is also seen as tolerant, but it was also merely the kings and emirs trying to prevent their image from being tarnished.

Individually these mechanisms were important, but once they are viewed together it will become apparent how the mirage of tolerance truly worked.

CHAPTER VI: IS TRUE TOLERANCE POSSIBLE?

Considering Spain is an often under-appreciated topic for historical study, Medieval Spain is one of the few topics that does get studied. For centuries, historians have been trying their best to understand the complex and unique situation of Spain in which three monotheistic religions lived among each other with some degree of tolerance. In the past fifty years, the major debate has been whether there was a complete tolerance as exhibited by the various tolerant laws, poetry, and the presence of many adoptions to the Spanish identity from Muslim and Jewish culture. However, there are also just as many negative and repressive laws in the legal libraries of Medieval Spain that have caused historians to think conversely that tolerance existed in no shape or form in Medieval Spain. Therefore, this study is vital to not conclusively answer the question, but to steer study in the proper direction.

Review

The way that this study is different from other studies is the fact that it proposes that there is a concept termed "the mirage of tolerance", and in this mirage of tolerance various aspects of Medieval Spanish history worked together to create the "mirage" (to historians and people of the time) that they were living in a tolerant world. That is not to say that some degree of true tolerance did not come out of this period. This true form of tolerance also goes by another term, which was coined around the early 1950s by historian Americo Castro. This specific term was *convivencia,* and the researcher is adapting this term to mean the natural adoption and acceptance of various aspects of someone else's culture deemed acceptable.[212] It is obvious from the poetry, architecture, and the language that Spaniards use today that some aspect of the more than seven hundred years that the Christians, Muslims, and Jews lived alongside each other exists. However, many historians, like Maria Rosa Menocal, have gone wrong in the past, when they assume that the whole period was tolerant. It requires the examination of the legal, financial, and militaristic aspects and motivations behind these Christian, Muslim, and Jewish societies. It was through the manipulation of these elements that the governments have fooled the people of the time and the historians of today.

Laws of Tolerance

The laws of tolerance include the various laws of Medieval Spain. These laws include two types of laws, the religious and the secular. The religious laws are important because it was these laws that created the groundworks of the psyche of the individuals of Medieval Spain. Christian religious laws require that Christians "love your neighbor as yourself…."[213] Muslim law in the Quran requires the Muslim to tolerate the "people of the book", which was anyone of Christian or Jewish religious belief.[214] Furthermore, the Jew was obligated to follow the laws set down in the Ten Commandments and various

---

[212] Novikoff, 20-24.

[213] Mark 12:31.

[214] Quran 3:64.

other laws in the Torah. Therefore, these religious laws created the natural behavior of the Christian, Muslim, and Jew in Medieval Spain. Therefore, when secular laws stated pay the jizya, a tax paid to the government of Spain to worship your specific religion, this law/tax automatically created a degree of tolerance between the individuals of Medieval Spain.[215] However, there was also the secular laws that further strengthened and made it so that the Christians, Muslims, and Jews of Medieval Spain were obligated to "tolerate" each other.

There were essentially three forms of legislations in Medieval Spain, and they all contributed to the way that people were controlled in Medieval Spain. There were the general laws of the town, village, or city. These were the "laws" in the sense that they controlled the way citizens behaved. Some of the most prominent laws worth mentioning include the "Pact of 'Umar", "The Treaty of Tudmir", and regulations on how the market should be laid out and conducted.[216] There were the *fueros,* which were laws that were slightly more elaborate and were usually used to establish laws for regions. The *fueros* were important because these laws give exact limits to what could and could not be done in the certain region in which a certain king or emir ruled. Many of these *fueros* were focused on the court systems, so, for example, the *Fuero* of Teruel describes when a Jew could represent himself in court.[217] There were also the law codes, which were usually

---

[215] Constable, 564.

[216] Lewis, 43; Al-Dabbi, 45-46; Ibn 'Abdun, 227-231.
[217] Strong, 320.

written and passed down to the public by kings or emirs. Two of the most popular law codes of this era were the *Usatges of Barcelona* and *Las Siete Partidas*. These law codes were written by kings, and they go into great detail about how the realms and kingdoms were to run, and how relations between Christian, Muslim, and Jew were to be followed. However, the main point of these forms of legal regulation was that they created a form of control that the Christian kings and Muslim emirs held over their subjects. There were repressive and "tolerant" laws in these law codes, but they all were utilized to create control over a large mass of people. The population of Spain was rather large during its medieval period; therefore, the government had to use legal control and obligatory tolerance to keep the people under control and avoid riot.

Money and Tolerance

Money, and having vast amounts of it, are critical for a kingdom or nation to be successful. Therefore, in Medieval Spain, it was paramount that Christian and Muslim Spain each were able to build up a strong, large treasury. It is understood that both Christian and Muslim Spain used basic means to gain money, but they also utilized certain strategies that took advantage of the citizens of Medieval Spain. These manipulative practices were utilized in a way that the citizens saw them as tolerant and accepting, but the practices were highly prejudiced and were primarily out of the intention to gain revenue from the people. The three main areas in which the governments of Medieval Spain used the people were the systems of tributes, the *Reconquista*, and the Inquisition.

Concerning the exploitation and manipulation of the tributes, the most prominent tribute was the *jizya*. This word is an Arabic word, and it was used to describe any tax or tribute paid to a Muslim government that allowed a Christian or Jew to practice their religion without molestation, for a small fee.[218] Although the Christians and Jews were minorities in Muslim Spain, the governments still profited from these tributes. According to sources, a city in a span of three years could owe, (in U.S. dollars) the equivalent to $3,795,600.[219] The people of the time, and some historians today, often take this to mean that the governments were being tolerant of the other religions. They were performing the obligatory rules that required them to, but in truth, they were using it as a source of income.

The Christian kings eventually utilized this tribute system during the *Reconquista* where they would conquer a city formerly owned by a Muslim emir/caliph, and then he would instruct the people that they did not need to leave because he would allow the freedom to worship, as long as they paid tribute. If one considers this idea, it only makes sense to keep the Muslims and Jews in the lands and obtain a profit from their presence. If a king were to force the Muslims and Jews to leave, that would be an extraordinary

---

[218] Constable, 91-92.

[219] Conversion tool, http://glossary.bahaiq.com/pages/mithqal.

source of income lost to the king. Furthermore, as the Christian kings re-conquered the lands lost to the Muslims in 711, they were able to gain more revenue, which was partially fueled by the use of the tributes of tolerance.

However, at a point, Muslims and Jews started to leave Christian lands, and the revenue from the tribute system was becoming thinner. Therefore, King Ferdinand and Queen Isabella instituted the Inquisition as another source of income for the Christian government of Spain. Originally, the Inquisition was established to judge the heretical individual. Therefore, for a very brief time, the Inquisition was not ridiculed as being intolerant. However, it quickly started to prosecute Muslims, Jews, and *conversos*. Therefore, this event did not continue the mirage of tolerance, but it inevitably destroyed the mirage and resulted in the expulsion of the Jews from Spain in 1492, and the Muslims ten years later.

Both Christian and Muslim Spain were nations competing for supremacy over the Iberian Peninsula. The only way to secure the supremacy was to make sure that they had a constant source of income. Therefore, they utilized the laws already established, and the tribute system to allow them to gain the ability to obtain large profits. However, this was done out of exploitation of the citizens. They were living their lives under the impression that their leaders were tolerant and caring, and the literature reflects that. Most histories of the medieval era describe the tolerance. However, in reality, the people were being manipulated.

War and Tolerance

The last part of this trifecta of illusion was the use of war and military strategy to create situations in which the Christian and Muslim governments of Spain could further prosper the illusion of tolerance. This was completed by a three-pronged strategy. The first was the use of alliances, pacts, and treaties. It was through these alliances, pacts, and treaties that military encounters could be delayed or stopped entirely for a mere yearly tribute to the gracious victor. However, these men were interested in their appearance; therefore, when the alliances, pacts, and tributes were developed, they were arranged in a way that the victor of the military strategy was gracious and tolerant. This can be seen in many alliances, pacts, and treaties where the victor makes it appear that he felt sorry for the poor mistreated Muslims and was willing to take them into his kingdom.[220]

Another strategy was the political intentions of the kings and emirs of Spain. This can be seen further in the situations where they team up with each other and take on a common enemy. Once again, historians for decades have been stating that this is a sign that tolerance did exist. It would be nearly impossible to prove whether there was true legitimate tolerance between the Christian and Muslim generals, but it does appear that they were joining in the alliances out of military strategy. They saw the opportunity as something that could get them the support of their Muslim or Christian subjects, or the

[220] Hernando del Pulgar, 496.

alliance could be an opportunity to delay war with the alliance member until an opportune moment.

The final strategy came from the *Reconquista*, in which the Christian kings were steadily taking up more and more land and creating more places and opportunities for the exploitation of the tribute system. People felt that they were being generously allowed to enter into a city with a tolerant king and live a life of peace. However, in reality, the government was making it so that they could grow and dominate over the enemies, which is a natural process of nation/kingdom building.

Putting it all Together

By now, it should be apparent that there is a degree of overlap in what is being termed the "mirage of tolerance." That is because, individually, the three aspects of the legal, financial, and military each have its own individual spheres of influence in Medieval Spain. However, these are the overlaps that go together to create the mirage of tolerance. What follows is a description of how the whole process of tolerance is created, and, in the end, what it was that destroyed the tolerance that existed in Medieval Spain.

Starting with the legal aspect, the laws were put into place to set up a degree of control over a large and growing population. As previously discussed, religious law created the idea that all should tolerate each other. From there the governments created laws that continued that idea. Many of these laws were developed and were associated with some fee or tax for tolerance to exist. Therefore, out of desire for more money, wealthy priests, kings, and emirs fought to institute many of these laws of tolerance. However, the arguing among each other for supremacy, also created animosity and agitation in Medieval Spain. Therefore, war was carried out, and from these wars, ideas such as the *Reconquista* and the Inquisition were created as ways to compete for superiority.

It has been discussed that tolerance could not exist in Medieval Spain because there was the constant presence of war and intolerance. To a degree, these claims are true because at any time in the near eight-hundred years of Muslim presence in Medieval Spain, the careful balance and usage of these mechanisms of tolerance were influenced. This is evident in the 1391 massacre of Jews in Spain. Jews were revolting against the intolerance that they were experiencing, and this caused "tolerance" to disappear. Conversely, times of "tolerance" are cited by historians such as Menocal, when 'Abd al-Rahman III promoted great translation efforts and poetry exhibitions. This worked because the perfect balance of the mechanisms was peaceful, and people were not being questioned over religion. It was during these times of simple close proximity that the true forms of tolerance formed.

These fragile mechanisms of control and balance also resulted in the destruction of the mirage of tolerance. For example, the *Reconquista* was created by the Christian kings to regain the lands lost to them from the Muslim conquests and to profit from the tributes that control over lands with Muslim and Jewish subjects. However, this *Reconquista* also strengthened and intensified ideas of prejudice and the ideas of one religion being superior to the other. Therefore, this caused that aspect of tolerance to fade. Furthermore, the creation of the Inquisition as a method to obtain money lost from the movement and migration of Jews and Muslims quickly turned into a visual display of tolerance. The people of Medieval Spain were being ingrained with prejudiced ideology, which obliterated any remnant of the mirage of tolerance. The final straw, however, was the expulsion of the Jews and Muslims. This was the "nail in the coffin" of tolerance in Medieval Spain.

Is True Tolerance Possible Today?

An investigation into the idea of tolerance may make a person wonder, is tolerance possible today? The U. S. Bill of Rights certainly states that "Congress shall make no law respecting an establishment of religion...."[221] This explicitly states that in the United States, there is no official religion. All religions are free to be practiced. However, that does not mean that people are not prejudiced and uneducated about the various religions of individuals living in America. Speaking in a more international scale, it is obvious that other nations have similar legislation, but that it still does not prevent the presence of intolerance. The term "tolerance" is a word that will never have a solid definition. The meaning of tolerance has changed through time to reflect society

---

[221] US Constitution, amend 1.

and its view at that specific time. In the twentieth century with the writings of Castro and Sanchez-Albornoz, in the topic of Medieval Spain, the term took on the meaning of the coexistence between Christians, Muslims, and Jews in Medieval Spain. However, in the twenty-first century, the term has taken on a meaning in which tolerance is a completely peaceful existence among the three parties. However, this idea is incorrect, and the definition has become flawed. Yet, trying to truly decipher the enigma of the term "tolerance" causes more questions than answers. Therefore, one needs to ask, is tolerance possible in this modern world, and how?

First there must be an explanation of the fact that there are two forms of tolerance. One form of tolerance is known as religious tolerance. It is this tolerance that is associated with whether people of different religions can live among each other despite their religious differences. These religious differences are not only delegated to whether Christians and Muslims can "tolerate" each other, but could also mean the schism between Muslims. This schism is reflected in the debate between the Shi'ia and the Sunni Muslims. Therefore, religious tolerance can become a very complicated topic of discussion. This view is complicated by the fact, that by focusing on the religious perspective, people may see with tunnel vision, and this causes the ideology that no other religion is better than the other. This ideology occurred during the eleventh to the fifteenth centuries in Medieval Spain. At this time, religion was central to the psyche, and this increase in religious prejudice destroyed the tolerance.

The other form of tolerance can be termed secular tolerance. This phrase means that people can live or work among each other in a setting that is not religiously fueled. This can describe locations like the work place, organizations, or competitive events. It is in these situations that people are focused on the situation at hand, and not purely focused on religious dogma. However, this ideology also has its weaknesses. One of the most prominent is the fact that secular tolerance pushes the ideology that religion does not matter and is insignificant to daily life. However, one cannot deny that there was a heightened degree of "tolerance" when Christians, Muslims, and Jews were working together to translate literature and creating poetry. They were not doing it because it was divinely ordained, but because it gave them pleasure and made them successful.

Therefore, the best strategy for tolerance would be to have a combination of the two ideas. Author Arvind Sharma has come up with two strategies to a way in which the two ideas can exist in a stable situation. Sharma states,

1. A neutral secularism which maintains the maximum separation between the state and religion…with no interference by the state except on manifest grounds of morality, health, and public order.
2. A positive secularism with the state intervention in the religious sphere which must be, and perceived to be, uniform in relation to all religions.[222]

Sharma is essentially stating that the primary idea of importance is the separation of church and state, which is an absolute must. The only time the interference is allowed is in the most important of situations, involving "morality, health, and public order."[223]

[222] Arvind Sharma, "Religious Tolerance in Three Contexts," *India International Cenre Quarterly* 22, no. 1 (Spring 1995): 34, accessed October 14, 2015, http://www.jstor.org/stable/23003709.

Furthermore, Sharma is stating that any interference into the religious sphere must be handled the exact same way regardless of religion. The reason that tolerance failed in Medieval Spain was because church and state were closely tied with each other, more so under Muslim Spain. Therefore, for a while the idea appeared to work, but eventually, intolerance and prejudiced ideas slipped into the common mentality.

However, the question still remains un-answered. Is tolerance possible today? If one examines the situation in the world, he/she will see a landscape that does not look good for a world of tolerance. In the Middle East, the debate over Shi'ia and Sunni ideology still rages on. A terrorist group ISIS is purposely targeting Christians, and a United States presidential candidate who calls for a wall of seclusion around a nation that has for centuries been the beacon of tolerance and acceptance. In Medieval Spain in 1492 King Ferdinand and Queen Isabella expelled the Jews from Spain, without much remorse. Presidential candidate Donald Trump speaks with the same ideology when he is proclaiming that immigrants have to leave without giving any plausible methodology. Unfortunately, tolerance *is* a mirage in modern times. Much like Medieval Spain laws, finances and war are methods to create the illusion of tolerance. In the Middle East, specifically in relation to the Gaza Strip, Christians, Muslims, and Jews try to share an area smaller than they did in Medieval Spain. Using the support of laws and money, there is a very fragile secular tolerance existing, but when any of those support systems

---

[223] Ibid.

falters, hell breaks loose. Sandra Marquart-Pyatt and Pamela Paxton point out an interesting view. They state that tolerance is found in education and understanding.[224] Until people learn how to appreciate each other for their humanness, tolerance will be impossible. Therefore, the only way to secure tolerance for the future would be to push the ideology of seeing each other as humans, and not Muslim or Christian. This succeeded in Medieval Spain when Christians, Muslims and Jews worked alongside each other to translate the ancient texts of old and enjoy poetry. One could logically argue that this view of tolerance is singular, and does not encompass the whole of society. However, change does not happen at once, but slowly and over a long period of time. Therefore, the only way for true tolerance to exist would be for the individual to change how they perceive the world, and slowly this idea would become the norm. When people no longer focus on how to be superior to someone, but learn how to live with someone, true tolerance will be born. In the end, tolerance is born one person at a time.

---

[224] Sandra Marquart-Pyatt and Pamela Paxton, 90,

BIBLIOGRAPHY

Primary Sources

'Abd Allah ibn Buluggin. Translated by Amin T. Tibi. "The Tibyan: Memoirs of 'Abd Alla ibn Buluggin, Last Zirid Amir of Granada." In *Medieval Iberia: Readings from Christian, Muslim, and Jewish Sources,* edited by Olivia Remie Constable, 117-122. Second Edition. Philadelphia, PA: University of Pennsylvania. 2012.

Ahmad Hijazi al-Saqqa, ed. Translated by Thomas E. Burman. "Al-I'lam bi-ma fi din al-nasara min al-fasad wa-awham wa-izhar mahasin din al islam wa-ithbat nubuwwat nabiyina Muhammade 'alayhi al-salat wa-al-salams." In *Medieval Iberia: Readings from Christian, Muslim, and Jewish Sources.* Edited by Olivia Remie Constable. Second Edition, 194-198. Philadelphia, PA: University of Pennsylvania Press. 2012.

Ahmad ibn 'Abd al-Samad al-Khazraji. Edited by 'Abd al-Majid al-Sharfi. Translated by Thomas E. Burman. "Maqami al-Sulban." In *Medieval Iberia: Readings from Christian, Muslim, and Jewish Sources.* Edited by Olivia Remie Constable. Second Edition, 190-194. Philadelphia, PA: University of Pennsylvania Press. 2012.

Al-Dabbi. Edited by Francisca Codera and Julian Ribera. Translated by Olivia Remie Constable"Kitab bughyat al-multamis fi ta'rikh rijal ahl al-Andalus." In *Medieval Iberia: Readings from Christian, Muslim, and Jewish Sources,* Edited by Olivia Remie Constable, 45-46. Second Edition. Philadelphia, PA: University of Pennsylvania Press. 2012.

Bastardis I Parera, Joan. Translated by Donald J. Kagay. *The Usatges of Barcelona: The Fundamental Law of Catalonia.* University of Pennsylvania Press. 2006. *The Library of Iberian Sources Online.* Accessed October 14, 2015. http://libro.uca.edu/usatges/opening.htm.

Beinart, Haim. "Records of the Trials of the Spanish Inquisition in Ciudad Real." In *The Spanish Inquisition, 1478-1614: An Anthology of Sources.* Edited by Lu Ann Homza, 13-16. Indianapolis, IN: Hackett Publishing Company, Ltd. 2006.

Burns, Robert I. ed and trans. *Middle Ages Series: Las Siete Partidas.* Volume 5. Philadelphia, PA: University of Pennsylvania Press. 2000.

------. trans. "Archive of the Crown of Aragon, Barcelona, cancilleria Real, Pergaminos de Jaume I, 734." Translated by Robert I. Burns. In *Medieval Iberia: Readings from Christian, Muslim, and Jewish Sources,* edited by Olivia Remie Constable, 279-280. Second Edition. Philadelphia, PA: University of Pennsylvania. 2012.

Burns, Robert and Paul Chevedden. eds and trans. "Negotiating Cultures: Bilingual Surrender Treaties in Muslim-Crusader Spain." In *Medieval Iberia: Readings from Christian, Muslim, and Jewish Sources,* edited by Olivia Remie Constable, 284-286. Second Edition. Philadelphia, PA: University of Pennsylvania Press. 2012.

Constable, Olivia Remie. ed. *Medieval Iberia: Readings from Christian, Muslim, and Jewish Sources.* Second Edition. PA: University of Pennsylvania Press. 2012.

De Pulgar, Hernando. Translated by Teofilo Ruiz. "Crónicas de los reyes de Castilla." In *Medieval Iberia: Readings from Christian, Muslim, and Jewish Sources,* edited by Olivia Remie Constable, 496-500. Second Edition. Philadelphia, PA: University of Pennsylvania Press. 2012.

Fernández y González, F. Translated by Dayle Seidenspinner-Nuñez. "Estado social y politico de los mudejares de Castilla." In *Medieval Iberia: Readings from Christian, Muslim, and Jewish Sources,* edited by Olivia Remie Constable, 535-539. Second Edition. Philadelphia, PA: University of Philadelphia Press. 2012.

Freedman, Paul. trans. "Vic, Arxiu Capitular, calaix 6, 22213, 27 April 1101." In *Medieval Iberia: Readings from Christian, Muslim and Jewish Sources,* edited by Olivia Remie Constable, 311-312. Second Edition. Philadelphia, PA: University of Pennsylvania Press. 2012.

------. trans. "Vic, Arxiu Capitular, calaix 7, 223, 23 December 1269." In *Medieval Iberia: Readings from Christian, Muslim, and Jewish Sources,* edited by Olivia Remie Constable, 313. Second Edition. Philadelphia, PA: University of Pennsylvania Press. 2012.

------. trans. "Vic, Arxiu Capitular, Liber dotationum antiquarum, folio 146v, 18 March 1212." In *Medieval Iberia: Readings from Christian, Muslim, and Jewish Sources,* edited by Olivia Remie Constable, 312-313. Second Edition. Philadelphia, PA: University of Pennsylvania Press. 2012.

Gomez-Moreno, Manuel and Juan de M. Carriazo. "Memorias del reinado de los Reyes catolicos, que escribe el bachiller Andres Bernaldez." In *The Spanish Inquisition, 1478-1614: An Anthology of Sources.* Edited and Translated by Lu Ann Homza. Indianapolis, IN: Hackett Publishing, Inc. 2006.

González, Julio. ed. Translated by James W. Brodman. "El reino de Castilla en la epoca de Alfonso VIII." In *Medieval Iberia: Readings from Christian, Muslim, and*

Jewish Sources, edited by Olivia Remie Constable, 208-209. Second Edition. Philadelphia, PA: University of Pennsylvania Press. 2012.

Goodenough, Anna. ed. and trans. "The Chronicle of Muntaner." In *Medieval Iberia: Readings from Christian, Muslim, and Jewish Sources,* edited by Olivia Remie Constable, 303-307. Second Edition. Philadelphia, PA: University of Pennsylvania Press. 2012.

Harvey, L. P. "Nubdhat al-'asr." In *Medieval Iberia: Readings from Christian, Muslim, and Jewish Sources,* edited by Olivia Remie Constable, 505-507. Second Edition. Philadelphia, PA: University of Pennsylvania Press. 2012.

Homza, Lu Ann. *The Spanish Inquisition, 1478-1614: An Anthology of Sources.* Indianapolis, IN: Hackett Publishing Inc. 2006.

Ibn 'Abd al Hakam. Edited by Charles C. Torrey. Translated by David A. Cohen. "Narrative the Conquest of Al-Andalus." In *Medieval Iberia: Readings from Christian, Muslim, and Jewish Sources.* Edited by Olivia Remie Constable. Philadelphia, PA: University of Pennsylvania Press. 2012.

Ibn Daud, Abraham. Translated by Gerson D Cohen. "The Book of Tradition." In *Medieval Iberia: Readings from Christian, Muslim, and Jewish Sources,* edited by Olivia Remie Constable, 91-92. Second Edition. Philadelphia, PA: University of Pennsylvania Press. 2012.

Ibn al-Qutiyya. Translated by Ann Christys. "Christians in Al-Andalus, 711-1000." In *Medieval Readings from Christian, Muslim, and Jewish Sources,* Edited by Olivia Remie Constable, 41-42. Second Edition. Philadelphia, PA: University of Pennsylvania Press. 2012.

Isidore of Seville. Translated by Kenneth B. Wolf. "History of the Goths, Vandals, and Suevi." In *Medieval Iberai: Readings from Christian, Muslim, and Jewish Sources.* Edited by Olivia Remie Constable, 3. Second Edition. Philadelphia, PA: University of Pennsylvania Press. 2012.

Klein, Elka. "Arxiu Capitular de Barcelona." In *Medieval Iberia: Readings from Christian, Muslim, and Jewish Sources.* Edited by Olivia Remie Constable, 339-342. Philadelphia, PA: University of Pennsylvania Press. 2012.

------. "Jews and Christians in Teruel: The Fuero of Teruel, 1176 CE." *Medieval Sourcebook.* Accessed October 9, 2015. https://legacy.fordham.edu/halsall/source/1276teruel.asp.

Lewis, Bernard. trans. "Islam from the Prophet Muhammad to the Capture of Constantinople." In *Medieval Iberia: Readings from Christian, Muslim, and Jewish Sources*, edited by Olivia Remie Menocal, 43-44. Second Edition. Philadelphia, PA: University of Pennsylvania Press. 2012.

Marcus, Jacob. *The Jew in the Medieval World: A Sourcebook, 315-1791.* New York: JPS. 1938. *Medieval Sourcebook.* Accessed October 9, 2015.

-----. ed. and trans. "Monumenta Germaniae Histoica: XIII, 3, 3." In *Medieval Iberia: Readings from Christian, Muslim, and Jewish Sources.* Edited by Olivia Remie Constable, 23-26. Philadelphia, PA: University of Pennsylvania Press. 2012.

Nelson, Lyn H. trans. "The Chronicle of San Juan de la Peña." In *Medieval Iberia: Readings from Christian, Muslim, and Jewish Sources,* edited by Olivia Remie Constable, 157-161. Second Edition. Philadelphia, PA: University of Pennsylvania Press. 2012.

O'Callaghan, Joseph, ed. and trans. "Cortes de los antiguas reinos de Leon y de Castilla." In *Medieval Iberia: Readings from Christian, Muslim, and Jewish Sources.* Edited by Olivia Remie Constable, 350. Philadelphia, PA: University of Pennsylvania Press. 2012.

Pidal, Ramón Menéndez. ed. Translated by John Moscatiello. "Primera crónica general de España." In *Medieval Iberia: Readings from Christian, Muslim, and Jewish Sources,* edited by Olivia Remie Constatble, 131-134. Second Edition. Philadelphia, Pennsylvania: University of Pennsylvania Press. 2012.

Powers, James F. trans. "The Code of Cuenca: Municipal Law on the Twelfth-Century Castilian Frontier." In *Medieval Iberia: Readings from Christian, Muslim, and Jewish Sources,* edited by Olivia Remie Constable, 221-224. Second Edition. Philadelphia, PA: University of Pennsylvania Press. 2012.

Ruiz, Juan. Edited by G. B. Gybbon-Moneypenny. Translated by Jill R. Webster. "Libro de buen amor." In *Medieval Iberia: Readings from Christian, Muslim, and Jewish Sources.* Edited by Olivia Remie Constable, 421-422. Philadelphia, PA: University of Pennsylvania Press. 2012.

Sesma Muñoz, J. Angel. "El establecimiento de la Inquisicion en Aragon." In *The Spanish Inquisition, 1478-1614: An Anthology of Sources.* Edited by Lu Ann Homza. Indianapolis, IN: Hackett Publishing Company, Ltd. 2006.

Scot, Samuel Parsons. ed. and trans. "Las siete partidas." In *Medieval Iberia: Readings from Christian, Muslim, and Jewish Sources,* edited by Olivia Remie Constable,

377-383. Second Edition. Philadelphia, PA: University of Pennsylvania Press. 2012.

Smith, Colin. ed. and trans. "Christians and Moors in Spain." vol. 1. In *Medieval Iberia: Readings from Christian, Muslim, and Jewish Sources,* edited by Olivia Remie Constable, 134-135. Second Edition. Philadelphia, PA: University of Pennsylvania Press. 2012.

Smith, Damian and Helena Buffery. trans. "The Book of Deeds of James I of Aragon: A Translation of the Medieval Catalan." In *Medieval Iberia: Readings from Christian, Muslims, and Jewish Sources,* edited by Olivia Remie Constable, 273-278. Second Edition. Philadelphia, PA: University of Pennsylvania Press. 2012.

Suárez-Fernández, Luis. ed. Translated by Edward Peters. "Documentos acerca de la expulsion de los judios." In *Medieval Iberia: Readings from Christian, Muslim, and Jewish Sources,* edited by Olivia Remie Constable, 508-513. Second Edition. Philadelphia, PA: University of Pennsylvania Press. 2012.

Wolf, Kenneth B. ed. and trans. "Conquerors and Chroniclers of Early Medieval Spain*".* In *Medieval Iberia: Readings from Christian, Muslim, and Jewish Sources*, edited by Olivia Remie Constable, 4. Second Edition. Philadelphia, PA: University of Pennsylvania Press. 2012.

Zeumer, Karl. ed. "Monumenta Germaniae Historica: Legum Sectio I, Leges Visigothorum." In *Medieval Iberia: Readings from Christian, Muslim, and Jewish Sources,* edited by Olivia Remie Constable, 24. Second Edition. Philadelphia, PA: University of Pennsylvania Press. 2012.

Secondary Sources

"Bahai Mithqal Calulator." Accessed November 1, 2015. http://glassary.bahaiq.com/pages/mithqal.

Carr, Raymond. *Spain: A History.* New York: Oxford University Press. 2000.

Davis, Gifford. "The Development of a National Theme in Medieval Castilian Literature." *Hispanic Review* 3, no. 2 (April 1935): 149-161. Accessed August 10, 2015. http://www.jstor.org/stable/469811.

Gerber, Jane S. *The Jews of Spain: A History of the Sephardic Experience.* New York: The Free Press. 1992.

Glick, Thomas F. and Oriol Pi-Sunyer. "Acculturation as an Explanatory Concept in Spanish History." *Comparative Studies* 11, no. 2 (April 1969): 136-154. Accessed August 11, 2015. http://www.jstor.org/stable/178249.

Goldschmidt Jr., Arthur and Lawrence Davidson. *A Concise History of the Middle East*, Tenth Edition. Boulder, CO: Westview Press. 2013.

Lea, Henry Charles. *A History of the Inquisition of Spain*. Volume 1-4. *The Library of Iberian Resources Online*. Accessed September 25, 2015. http://libro.uca.edu/lea/opening.htm.

Lowney, Chris. *A Vanished World: Muslims, Christians, and Jews in Medieval Spain*. New York: Oxford University Press. 2005.

Marquart-Pyatt, Sandra and Pamela Paxton. "In Principle and in Practice: Learning Political Tolerance in Eastern and Western Europe." *Political Behavior* 29, no. 1 (March 2007): 89-113. Accessed October 14, 2015. http://www.jstor.org/stable/4500235.

Menocal, María Rosa. *The Ornament of the World: How Muslims, Jews, and Christians Created a Culture of Tolerance in Medieval Spain*. New York: Back Bay Books. 2002.

Novikoff, Alex. "Between Tolerance and Intolerance in Medieval Spain: An Historiographic Enigma." *Medieval Encounters* 11, no. 2 (2005): 7-36.

O'Callaghan, Joseph F. *A History of Medieval Spain*. New York: Cornell University Press. 1983.

Russel, Josiah C. "Tables on Population in Medieval Europe." *Medieval Sourcebook*. Accessed October 5, 2015. http://legacy.fordham.edu/halsall/source/pop-in-eur.asp.

Sharma, Arvind. "Religious Tolerance in Three Contexts." *India International Centre Quarterly* 22, no. 1 (1995): 29-34. Accessed October 14, 2015. http://www.jstor.org/stable/23003709.

Strong, Wm. T. "The Fueros of Northern Spain." *Political Science Quarterly* 8, no. 2 (June 1893): 317-334. Accessed October 14, 2015. http://www.jstor.org/stable/2139647.

Made in the USA
Las Vegas, NV
05 March 2022

45059618R00070